The Aquinas Lecture, 1980

DOES GOD HAVE A NATURE?

Under the auspices of the
Wisconsin-Alpha Chapter of Phi Sigma Tau

By
ALVIN PLANTINGA, Ph.D.

42-005

MARQUETTE UNIVERSITY PRESS
MILWAUKEE
1980

Library of Congress Catalog Number 80-65854

© Copyright 1980
Marquette University

ISBN 0-87462-145-3

PRINTED
IN
U.S.A.

Prefatory

The Wisconsin-Alpha Chapter of Phi Sigma Tau, the National Honor Society for Philosophy at Marquette University, each year invites a scholar to deliver a lecture in honor of St. Thomas Aquinas.

The 1980 Aquinas Lecture *Does God Have a Nature?* was delivered in the Todd Wehr Chemistry Building on Sunday, February 24, 1980, by Alvin Plantinga, Professor of Philosophy at Calvin College, Grand Rapids, Michigan.

After completing his undergraduate studies at Calvin College, Professor Plantinga earned an M.A. at the University of Michigan in 1955 and a Ph.D. at Yale University in 1958. He taught at Yale University and Wayne State University before returning to Calvin College in 1963 where he became Professor of Philosophy in the following year. He has been a visiting lecturer at the University of Illinois and Harvard University and visiting professor at the University of Chicago, the University of Michigan, Boston University, Indiana University, UCLA, and Notre Dame.

Dr. Plantinga edited *Faith and Philosophy*, 1964, and *The Ontological Argument*, 1965. He is the author of *God and Other Minds*, 1967, *The Nature of Necessity*, 1974, and *God, Freedom and Evil*, 1974. His published articles number over forty and have appeared in *Philosophical Studies*, *Theoria*, *American Philosophical Quarterly*, *Canadian Journal of Philosophy*, *New Scholasticism*, *Review of Metaphysics*, *Journal of Philosophy*, *Reformed Journal*, *Philosophical Review*, *Nous*, and other distinguished journals and books.

Dr. Plantinga was a Guggenheim Fellow in 1971 and 1972. He has been a member of the American Academy of Arts and Sciences since 1975; he was a Visiting Fellow at Balliol College, Oxford in 1975-1976. Amid all his intellectual pursuits, he finds time for his avocation of mountaineering and rock climbing.

To Professor Plantinga's distinguished list of publications, Phi Sigma Tau is pleased to add: *Does God Have a Nature?*

Does God Have a Nature?

Introduction

Christians think of God as a being of incomparable greatness. He is the first being of the universe, one than whom it is not so much as possible that there be a greater. God's greatness is not just one step—even a big step—further along a scale measuring the greatness of things in general; his greatness is of a different order from that of his creatures. If the ordinary cardinal numbers—finite and infinite—measure *our* greatness then God must be compared to an inaccessible cardinal (though that might make him sound too much like an unduly reclusive candidate for Pope). God's greatness has many facets; preeminent among them are his love, justice, mercy, power and knowledge. As important as any, however, are his *aseity*—his uncreatedness, self-sufficiency and independence of everything else—and his *sovereignty*—

his control over all things and the dependence of all else on his creative and sustaining activity. Most Christians claim that God is the uncreated creator of all things; all things depend on him, and he depends upon nothing at all.

Now the created universe presents no problem for this doctrine. Mountains, planets, stars, quarks, you and I and all the rest of us—we have all been created by God and we exist at his sufferance. On the other hand, he does not depend on us, either for his existence or for his properties. True, he accords some of his creatures *freedom*, and thus may be thought dependent, in a Pickwickian fashion, on their free actions. He may have certain aims and goals which can be attained only with the free and uncoerced cooperation of his creatures. But even here, every free action and hence every act of rebellion against him and his precepts is totally dependent upon him. Our every act of rebellion has his sustaining activity as a necessary substratum; the rebel's very existence depends from moment to moment on God's affirming activity. "The power, even of those who are hurtful," says Augustine, "is from God alone." This dependence upon God is not something we may hope one day to outgrow. Perhaps human technology will someday overcome suffering, want, disease and, conceivably, death itself: perhaps so and perhaps not. But even if so, to declare ourselves independent of God would be at best a piece of laughable bravado; for the very causal laws on which we rely in any activity are no more than the record of God's regular, constant and habitual dealings with the stuff of the universe he has created.

So God's creation creates no special problem here: it is dependent on him in myriad ways; he is in no way significantly dependent upon it. What does or might seem to create a problem are not these creatures of God, but the whole realm of abstract objects—the whole Platonic pantheon of universals, properties, kinds, propositions, numbers, sets, states of affairs and possible worlds. It is natural to think of these things as *everlasting*, as having neither beginning nor end. There was a time before which there were no human beings, but no time before which there was not such a thing as the property of being human or the proposition *there are human beings*. That property and that proposition have always existed and have never *begun* to exist. Abstract objects are also naturally thought of as *necessary* features of reality, as objects whose non-existence is impossible. There could have been no mountains or planets; but could there have been no such thing as the property of being a mountain or the proposition *there are nine planets?* That proposition could have been *false*, obviously, but could it have been *non-existent?* It is hard to see how. Sets of contingent objects, perhaps, are as contingent as their members; but properties, propositions, numbers and states of affairs, it seems, are objects whose non-existence is quite impossible.

If so, however, how are they related to God? According to Augustine, God created everything distinct from him; did he then create these things?

Presumably not; they have no beginnings. Are they dependent on him? But how could a thing whose non-existence is impossible—the number 7, let's say, or the property of being a horse—depend upon anything for its existence? And what about the characteristics and properties these things display? Does God (so to speak) just find them constituted the way they are? Must he simply put up with their being thus constituted? Are these things, their existence and their character, outside his control? Augustine saw in Plato a *vir sapientissimus et eruditissimus* (*Contra Academicos* III, 17); yet he felt obliged to transform Plato's theory of ideas in such a way that these abstract objects become, obscurely, *part* of God—perhaps identical with his intellect. It is easy to see why Augustine took such a course, and easy to see why most later medieval thinkers adopted similar views. For the alternative seems to *limit* God in an important way; the existence and necessity of these things distinct from him seems incompatible with his sovereignty.

And what about his own properties—
omnipotence, justice, wisdom and the
like? Did he create them? But if God has
created wisdom, then he existed before it
did, in which case, presumably, there
was a time at which he was not wise. But
surely he has *always* been wise; he has
not *acquired* wisdom. Furthermore, he
seems to be somehow conditioned and
limited by these properties, and dependent upon them. Take the property *omniscience* for example. If that property
didn't exist, then God wouldn't have it,
in which case he wouldn't be omniscient.
So the existence of omniscience is a necessary condition of God's being the way he
is; in this sense he seems to be dependent
upon it. Omniscience, furthermore, has
a certain character: it is such that
whoever has it, knows, for any proposition p, whether or not p is true. But its
displaying this character is not up to God
and is not within his control. God did not
bring it about that omniscience has this
character, and there is no action he could
have taken whereby this property would
have been differently constituted.

Neither its existence nor its character seems to be within his control. Furthermore, its existence and its having the character it does are necessary conditions of God's being the way *he* is. But how is this compatible with his being truly sovereign? In this way God seems to be limited and conditioned by the properties he has.

Still further, suppose God has a *nature*—a property he has essentially that includes each property essential to him.[1] Perhaps God is essentially omniscient; that is, perhaps it's just not possible that he fail to be omniscient. If so, then it isn't up to him whether he has that property; his having it is in no way

---

1. One property includes another if it is not possible that there be an object that has the first but not the second. Thus the property of being a horse includes the property of being an animal. The nature of an object can be thought of as a conjunctive property, including as conjuncts just those properties essential to that object. Accordingly, an object has a nature if it has any essential properties at all. For more about natures, see my book *The Nature of Necessity* (Oxford: Oxford University Press, 1974), Chapter V.

dependent upon his own decision or will.
He simply finds himself with it; and that
he has it is in no way up to him. So God's
having a nature seems incompatible with
his being in total control. As Hendrick
Hart says,

> As far as I can see, a view that commits one
> to holding that God is subject to laws
> (exemplifies predicables) that are neither
> created by him nor identical with him, is a
> view that commits one to holding that God
> is neither sovereign nor omnipotent.[2]

If abstract objects such as propositions
and properties are necessarily existent,
then affirming their existence and knowing that they exist will be part of God's
nature—at any rate if omniscience is. If
God is essentially omniscient, then for
any abstract object you pick, that object
will be a necessary being only if it is part
of God's nature to know of and affirm its
existence. So our questions can be put
this way: does God have a nature? And if

2. "On the Distinction Between Creator and
Creature," *Philosophia Reformata*, 1979, p. 184.

he does, is there a conflict between God's sovereignty and his having a nature? How is God related to such abstract objects as properties and propositions? These are the questions I want to explore.

These questions may sound unduly recondite or even a bit arcane to contemporary ears. The fact is, however, that nearly all of the great theistic thinkers of the past have addressed them, and for good reason: they are crucially important for any deep understanding of what it is to see God as the sovereign first being of the universe. In Part I I shall argue that there is no good reason to think these questions cannot sensibly be addressed. In Part II I shall consider the answer given by Thomas Aquinas and others: God has a nature, all right, but he is *identical* with it, so that he is not limited and conditioned by something distinct from him. In Part III I shall take up nominalism, the view that God has no nature because there are no natures to be had; there are no properties at all. In Part IV I shall discuss Descartes' *univer-*

sal possibilism, according to which God
has no nature, not because there are no
properties but because he has no properties essentially. These answers, I argue,
should all be rejected; and in Part V I de-
fend what I take to be the simple truth:
God has a nature which is not identical
with him.

I. Can We Discuss the Question?

What are the options here available to
the theist? One possibility is to reject the
whole question. A view widely held by
contemporary theologians is that our
conceptual scheme—our categories and
concepts—applies only within the world
of experience or the "temporal horizon";
hence it does not apply to God. The proximate source for this notion is Immanuel
Kant, who has much to answer for in this
connection as in several others. Kant said
many things, not all of them clearly compatible. But among the things he said is
that such fundamental concepts or categories as those of *negation* and *substance-
property* have application only within
the world of experience or the world of

appearance; they do not apply to things as they are in themselves, apart from the conceptual activity of human beings. In "synthesizing the manifold," as he put it, we construct the world of appearance out of the raw material of experience; and we construct it in terms of the categories. Thus we construct a world in which there are things that have properties and things to which the category of negation applies. We are thus constrained to think of the world as composed of things that have properties; we are obliged to think in terms of an object-property structure. But this category, this aspect of our conceptual scheme, has its origins in *us*; and it makes no sense to suppose that it applies to things in themselves. *We* are obliged thus to think; but why suppose reality as such, independent of our noetic activity, is under any obligation to conform to this structure? Our categories are properly applicable within the realm of appearance—a realm that owes its basic contours to our own formative activity. To try to apply them beyond the world of appearance to the realm of reality is to employ reason in an area where it cannot profitably venture; it is to fall victim to *Transzendental Schein*.

But if our categories do not apply to the realm of reality or things in themselves, then they do not apply to God, who is a thing in himself *in excelsis*. And if our categories do not apply to God, then the thing-property category and the category of negation do not apply to God. Hence we cannot sensibly claim that God has a nature; to do so is to suppose that he has properties and that the thing-property category applies to him. But neither can we sensibly claim that God does *not* have a nature; for to do so is to apply the category of negation to him. If our categories and concepts do not apply to God, we can't so much as sensibly raise the question whether he has a nature or properties, or how he is related to them. If these Kantian claims are true, we must remain totally agnostic with respect to this question—or better, we must reject the whole question as naively presupposing that our categories apply beyond the realm of experience.

Now Kant clearly teaches that our concepts do not apply to God. Of course he also seems to teach that some at least, of our concepts *do* apply to God; this is part of his charm. But the agnostic teaching is what has historically had the greatest impact and what is presently relevant; these Kantian ideas have enjoyed enormous popularity in recent theology. Tillich held that ordinary theism must be transcended, that we must suppose the fundamental reality is a God beyond God to whom none of our concepts and categories—not even existence—applies. And many contemporary theologians follow him here. Gordon Kaufman, for example, finds the idea of God problematic; indeed, he has written a book entitled *God the Problem.*[3] Why is God a problem for Kaufman?

The central problem of theological dis-

---

3. Cambridge: Harvard University Press, 1972. Page references to Kaufman's work are to this volume.

course, not shared with any other "language game," is the meaning of the term "God." "God" raises special problems of meaning because it is a noun which by definition refers to a reality transcendent of, and thus not locatable within, experience. A new convert may wish to refer the "warm feeling" in his heart to God, but God is hardly to be identified with this emotion; the biblicist may regard the Bible as God's Word; the moralist may believe God speaks through men's consciences; the churchman may believe God is present among his people—but each of these would agree that God himself transcends the locus referred to. As the Creator or Source of all that is, God is not to be identified with any particular finite reality; as the proper object of ultimate loyalty or faith, God is to be distinguished from every proximate or penultimate value or being. But if absolutely nothing within our experience can be directly identified as that to which the term "God" properly refers, what meaning does or can the word have? (8).

Here the problem seems to be that God is not identical with any finite reality (which is true) and hence is not identical with anything of which we have experience (which does not follow). And the

implied suggestion is that if an allegedly
denoting term does not denote something
of which we have experience, then there
is a problem about what it denotes, if indeed, it denotes anything. Kaufman's
suggested solution to this alleged problem is a striking echo of Kant's agnosticism with respect to God. And the heart
of his alleged solution is a distinction he
makes between the "real" referent of the
term 'God' and what he calls the "available" referent:

> The real referent for "God" is never accessi-
> ble to us or in any way open to our observa-
> tion or experience. It must remain always
> an unknown X, a mere limiting idea with
> no content (85).

> God is ultimately profound Mystery and
> utterly escapes our every effort to grasp or
> comprehend him. Our concepts are at best
> metaphors and symbols of his being, not
> literally applicable (95).

So the real referent of the term 'God' is
not available to us; our concepts do not
apply to it; it is utterly beyond our ken.
But what about the things Christians say
of God—that He is almighty, all-know-

ing, faithful, that he created and sustains the world, loves his children, has redeemed mankind and the world in the death and resurrection of his Son? When Christians speak thus, says Kaufman, they are speaking not of the real referent of the name 'God,' but of its "available referent";

> For all practical purposes, it is the *available referent*—a particular imaginative construct—that bears significantly on human life and thought. It is the "available God" whom we have in mind when we worship or pray; . . . it is the available God in terms of which we speak and think whenever we use the word "God." In this sense "God" denotes for all practical purposes what is essentially a mental or imaginative construct (86).

> Does this mean, then, that the conclusion is, after all, that God really does not exist, that He is only a figment of our imaginations? If these words are intended to put the speculative question about the ultimate nature of things, then, as we have seen, there is no possible way to give an answer (111).

In essence, then, Kaufman's view ap-

DOES GOD HAVE A NATURE? 17

pears to be the following. The term 'God'
has an available referent; this is a human
construction, something we have created. Perhaps it also has a real referent,
although it is impossible to know
whether in fact there is any such thing. If
there is, however, it transcends our experience and is hence something to which
our concepts do not apply—a mere
unknown X, to adopt Kaufman's Kantian terminology.

This position, I believe, displays confu
sion. In particular, I think Kaufman con-
fuses the denotation of the term 'God'
with a set of properties expressed by or
otherwise associated with that term. But
what is relevant to our present concerns is
the claim that God Himself—what Kaufman calls "the real referent"—is such
that our concepts do not apply to him, so
that we cannot so much as raise the question whether he has a nature. At any
rate, Kaufman's words clearly suggest
this claim. Of course appearances can
be deceiving; perhaps he does not mean
to commit himself to it; perhaps he is to
be understood in some other way. I am

less concerned to ascribe this view to him than to explore the view itself. And from a theistic point of view this claim, I believe, is totally untenable, both philosophically and theologically.

But before I explain why I think so, we must carefully distinguish the claim in question from two others. In the first place, it must not be confused with the truth that our knowledge of God is bound to be limited, fragmentary, halting and inchoate. What we know about God must be miniscule indeed in comparison with what we do not know; furthermore, there must be a great deal about him of which we can form no conception at all. But of course this truth is compatible with our knowing *something* about God—that he exists and created the world and loves us, for example. This truth does not at all imply that none of our concepts apply to God; what it implies is only that God has many properties of which we do not have concepts. Hence this truth does not imply that we cannot sensibly raise the question whether God has a nature.

Secondly, the claim in question must be distinguished from the traditional *via negativa*. According to this idea, what we can know of God is essentially negative; there are no properties such that we know of them that God has them, although there are some properties we know he *lacks*. Those who held this view were committed to supposing that properties are all positive in nature and typically do not have complements. On this view, there is such a thing as the property of being a horse, but no such thing as the property of not being a horse. Furthermore, many predicates will not express properties. 'Is blind,' for example, does not express a property; when we say 'Homer is blind,' we do not ascribe a property to Homer, but rather deny that he has the property of being sighted. But whatever the merits of this idea, those who held it did not suppose that we cannot raise the question whether God has a nature; they raised it and answered affirmatively. Nor did they suppose that we cannot apply the category of negation, for example, to God; they regularly applied it in denying various properties of him.

So both of these views must be distinguished from the claim that our concepts do not apply to God. But how shall we understand this claim? What might it mean to say that our concepts don't apply to God? To answer this question, we must ask another: what is it to have a concept? To say that someone has the concept of being a horse is to say that she grasps or understands or apprehends the property *being a horse*.[4] To say she has the concept of prime number is to say she grasps or apprehends the property *being a prime number;* she knows what it is for something to be a prime number. Some properties, clearly enough, aren't understood or grasped by everyone; some people have concepts others lack. Small children typically don't know what it is for a number to be prime; large philosophers often don't grasp such properties as, say, *being a quark*. We have concepts corresponding to those properties we grasp or apprehend. Furthermore, apprehending a property is a matter of degree. You and I may have *some* grasp of the property *being a quark;* a physicist, we hope, will have a better grasp.

And what is it for one of my concepts to *apply* to something? Here the answer is satisfyingly obvious. I have the concept *horse* if I grasp the property of being a horse; and that concept *applies to* something if that thing is a horse, has the property of being a horse. Our concept *being a horse* applies to each thing that

---

4. Of course putting it this way implies that if we say someone has the concept of being a horse, then we are committed to supposing that there is such a *property* as *being a horse.* Someone suspicious of properties might demur: he might hold that while indeed many people have concepts, there aren't any properties. To accommodate those with nominalistic leanings, therefore, we may put the matter thus: to have the concept of being a horse is to know what horses are, to know what it is to be a horse. In what follows I shall continue to assume that there are properties and that knowing what it is to be a horse is to grasp the property of being a horse. Nothing I say, however, will be essentially dependent upon this assumption; all of what I want to say can be recast in that more nominalistic fashion.

has the property of being a horse; my
concept of prime number applies to all
the prime numbers.

Now suppose we return to the question
whether our concepts apply to God. It is
a piece of sheer confusion to say that
there is such a person as God, but none of
our concepts apply to him. If our concepts do not apply to God, then he does
not have such properties as *wisdom, being almighty* and *being the creator of the
heavens and the earth*. Our concept of
wisdom applies to a being if that being is
wise; so a being to whom this concept did
not apply would not be wise, whatever
else it might be. If, therefore, our concepts do not apply to God, then our concepts of being loving, almighty, wise,
creator and Redeemer do not apply to
him, in which case he is not loving,
almighty, wise, a creator or a Redeemer.
He won't have any of the properties
Christians ascribe to him. In fact he
won't have any of the properties of which
we have concepts. He will not have such
properties as self-identity, existence, and
being either a material object or an im-

material object, these being properties of
which we have concepts. Indeed, he
won't have the property of being the
referent of the term 'God,' or any other
term; our concept *being the referent of a
term* does not apply to him. The fact is
this being won't have any properties at
all, since our concept of having at least
one property does not apply to him. But
how could there be such a thing? How
could there be a being that didn't exist,
wasn't self-identical, wasn't either a
material object or an immaterial object,
didn't have any properties? Does any of
this make even marginal sense? It is
clearly quite impossible that there be a
thing to which none of our concepts
apply.

And what, besides the example of
Kant, might prompt someone to hold
such an extraordinary view? Perhaps an
argument of the following sort:

  (1) God transcends human experience;
       we cannot observe or in any other
       way experience him.

Therefore:

  (2) Our concepts do not apply to God.

This inference is doubly defective, and
defective in an instructive fashion. In the
first place, (1) clearly says something
about God: that he transcends human
experience. So one who offers this argument must suppose that God transcends
human experience. She also supposes,
clearly enough, that we do have some
grasp of what it is to transcend human
experience; else how would she know (as
she thinks she does know) that if God
transcends human experience, then (2) is
true? So the person who offers this argument must suppose both that God transcends human experience, and that we
know what it is to transcend human experience. But if those suppositions are
true, then at least one of our concepts
does apply to God: in which case (2), the
conclusion of the argument, is false. So
one who seriously offers this argument is
committed to holding that its conclusion
is false; and this means the argument
cannot coherently be advanced. And this
difficulty, obviously enough, attaches
itself to any attempt to argue for (2). Any
argument for (2) will have to specify

some property *P* God has—a property in virtue of which our concepts don't apply to God. But then one who offers the argument must suppose both that we have the concept of *P* and that this concept applies to God, so that the argument collapses into self-referential incoherence.

Secondly, the conclusion (2) itself cannot coherently be maintained. For one who maintains it says something about God: that our concepts do not apply to him. He must therefore suppose that God has that property. And if he is serious about maintaining or asserting (2), he must suppose that some of us, at any rate, grasp or apprehend what it is for a thing to be such that our concepts do not apply to it. Accordingly, we have the concept *being such that none of our concepts applies to it*. If (2) is true, this concept applies to God. But then at least one of our concepts does apply to God, in which case (2) is false. So one who maintains or asserts (2) is committed to supposing that (2) is false—but also, of course, that it is true. Hence one cannot coherently assert (2).

And this is just a special case of a more general malady afflicting any view of which (2) is a consequence. This way of thinking begins in a pious and commendable concern for God's greatness and majesty and augustness; but it ends in agnosticism and in incoherence. For if none of our concepts apply to God, then there is nothing we can know or truly believe of him—not even what is affirmed in the creeds or revealed in the Scriptures. And if there is nothing we can know or truly believe of him, then, of course, we cannot know or truly believe that none of our concepts apply to him. The view that our concepts don't apply to God is fatally ensnarled in self-referential absurdity. We cannot sensibly respond to our question then—the question whether God has a nature—by dismissing it as naively presupposing that our concepts apply to God.

II. Divine Simplicity

Historically the most widely accepted answer to our question is *Yes*. God does

indeed have a nature; but he is identical
with it. God is somehow simple, utterly
devoid of complexity. He has a nature;
but he and it are the very same thing. But
then of course it is not prior to him; and
if he is dependent upon it, this is no more
than a harmless case of self-dependence.
This mysterious doctrine has its roots
deep in antiquity, going all the way back
to Parmenides, with his vision of reality
as an undifferentiated plenum in which
no distinctions can be made. The idea
that God is simple has been embraced by
thinkers as diverse as Duns Scotus and
Louis Berkhof; it is to be found both in
the ancient creeds of the church and in
such relatively recent declarations as the
Belgic Confession.

The basic idea of this doctrine is that
no distinctions can be made in God. We
cannot distinguish him from his nature,
or his nature from his existence, or his
existence from his other properties; he is
the very same thing as his nature, existence, goodness, wisdom, power and the
like. And this is a dark saying indeed.

The difficulty is two-fold. In the first
place, it is exceedingly hard to grasp or
construe this doctrine, to see just what
divine simplicity *is*. Secondly, insofar as
we do have a grasp of this doctrine, it is
difficult to see why anyone would be inclined to accept it; the motivation for this
doctrine seems shrouded in obscurity.
Why should anyone want to hold that
God just is the same thing as, say,
goodness? Why hold that no distinctions
can be made in God? Suppose we start
with this second perplexity.

1. Why Simplicity?

When Thomas Aquinas embarks on
the task of characterizing God's attri-
butes, simplicity is the first item on his
list.[5] He is quite clear, furthermore, as to
his reasons for holding this doctrine; the
fundamental reason is to accommodate
God's aseity and sovereignty. Aquinas

---

5. *Summa Theologiae* (hereafter ST) Ia, Question 3.

believes that if God had a nature and properties distinct from him, then there would be beings distinct from him to which he is subsequent and on which he depends; this would compromise his aseity and ill befits the status of the First Being. "Secondly," he says, "everything composite is subsequent to its components and dependent upon them; whilst God, as we have seen, is the first of all beings."[6] But how or why is a thing *dependent* on its components? What is it for a thing to be *subsequent* to its components? And what sorts of things does Aquinas think of as components of an object? The spatial parts of a material object, he thinks, are components of it; the *nature* or essence of an object is a component of it, as are its existence and any other property—essential or accidental—it may have.

So a fundamental—perhaps *the* fun-

---

6. ST Ia, 3, 8; see also *Summa Contra Gentiles* (hereafter SCG), I, 18, 3.

damental—reason for simplicity doctrine is that it seems implied by God's
sovereignty and aseity. But why should
an object be thought of as dependent on
its properties? Aquinas clearly says *that*
this is so; he is less explicit as to why.
Among a thing's properties is its nature
or essence. But the essence of an object he
holds,

> is either the thing itself or related to the
> thing in some way as its cause; for a thing
> derives its species through its essence. But
> nothing can in any way be the cause of
> God, since as we have shown, He is the first
> being (SCG I, 21, 5).

If an object is distinct from its essence,
then its essence is in some way a *cause*
of that thing, so that the latter is dependent—causally dependent—on the
former. Aquinas argues that the same
considerations apply to a thing's
goodness, existence and, by implication,
any other properties it may have. For
example,

> . . . anything that exists either is itself exist-
> ence or is a being [existent] by participa-
> tion. Now God, as we have seen, exists. If

> then he is not himself existence, and thus
> not by nature existent, he will be a being
> [existent] only by participation. And so he
> will not be the first being (ST Ia, 3, 4).

And

> . . . each good thing that is not its goodness
> is called good by participation. But that
> which is named by participation has some-
> thing prior to it from which it receives the
> character of goodness. This cannot proceed
> to infinity, since among final causes there is
> no regress to infinity . . . We must therefore
> reach some first good, that is not by partici-
> pation good through an order towards some
> other good, but is good through its own
> essence. This is God. God is therefore His
> own goodness (SCG I, 38).

In the same way God is his wisdom, his
knowledge, his blessedness, and each of
the rest of his virtues.

The essential idea, then, is that if God
were good, or blessed, or knowledgable
or wise by *participation* in the properties
goodness, knowledge, blessedness, or
wisdom, then he would be *subsequent* to
these properties; and if he *had* an essence
(or nature), as opposed to being *identical*
with it, then that essence would be his

cause. These two considerations are linked in the last passage, which suggests that if a thing has a property by participation (by having it without being identical with it) then *it is subsequent to that property in the order of final causation*. And what this means, I think, is the following. If God were distinct from such properties as wisdom, goodness and power but nonetheless *had* these properties, then he would be *dependent* on them. He would be dependent on them in a dual way. First, if, as Aquinas thinks, these properties are essential to him, then it is not possible that he should have existed and they not be 'in' him. But if they had not existed, they could not have been in him. Therefore he would not have existed if they had not. This connection between his existence and theirs, furthermore, is necessary; it is not due to his will and it is not within his power to abrogate it. That it holds is not up to him or within his control. He is obliged simply to put up with it. No doubt he wouldn't *mind* being thus constrained, but that is not the point. The point is that he would be dependent upon something else for his existence, and dependent in a way outside his control and beyond his power to alter; this runs counter to his aseity.

Secondly, under the envisaged conditions God would be dependent upon these properties for his character. He is, for example, *wise*. But then if there had been no such thing as wisdom, he would not have been wise. He is thus dependent upon these properties for his being the way he is, for being what he is like. And again he didn't bring it about that he is thus dependent; this dependence is not a result of his creative activity; and there is nothing he can do to change or overcome it. If he had properties and a nature distinct from him, then he would exist and display the character he does display because of a relation in which he stands to something other than himself. And this doesn't fit with his existence *a se*. Aquinas therefore concludes that these properties are indeed 'in' God, but in such a way that he is identical with them. He just is his nature.

Now I think the intuition—call it the sovereignty-aseity intuition—underlying the doctrine of divine simplicity must be taken with real seriousness. Suppose God has essentially the property of being omnipotent and suppose that property is an object distinct from him, is uncreated by him and exists necessarily. Then in some sense he does depend on that property. For in the first place he could not have existed if it had not; its existence is a necessary condition of his existence. And secondly he couldn't have the character he does have, couldn't be the way he is, if omnipotence didn't exist or weren't the way *it* is. If omnipotence were of a different character—if, for example, it couldn't be *had* by anything, or were such that nothing could both have it and be wise—then God would not have existed or would not have been the way he is: either he wouldn't have been omnipotent or he wouldn't have been wise. Further, this connection between him and the nature and existence of omnipotence is not owing to his decision or activity; nor is it within his power to cancel or alter it. And, initially, at least, this seems incompatible with his aseity.

Still further, we have been speaking only of his own properties; but of course there is the rest of the Platonic menagerie—the propositions, properties, numbers, sets, possible worlds and all the rest. If these things are distinct from God, if they exist necessarily and have their characters essentially, then there is a vast and enormous structure that seems to be independent of God. That there are natural numbers, for example, is not up to God; he didn't create them and couldn't destroy them. They do not owe their character to him. The properties they have and the relations in which they stand are not within his control. So if God has a nature distinct from him, then there are things distinct from him on which he depends; and if the rest of the Platonic menagerie are distinct from him, then there are innumerable beings whose existence and character are independent of God. And doesn't it seem that this compromises his sovereignty?

That this swarm of Platonic parapher-

nalia infringes on the sovereignty of God
is the best argument I know for nominalism. God exists, is the sovereign first
being, depends upon nothing else and is
such that everything else depends on
him; if there were such things as properties, numbers, propositions and the rest
of the Platonic *melange*, they would exist
necessarily and have their properties
essentially; but then there would be an
uncountable host of beings intuitively
independent of God on some of which he
depends. So there aren't any such things.
Surely this is a better argument for nominalism than any based on a hankering for
ontological penury or a taste for desert
landscapes. After all, the Olympic penin-
sula is just as impressive as the Sonora
desert. The theistic argument for nominalism is at any rate based on more than
personal preference. If the Platonic pantheon infringes on the divine sovereignty,
perhaps we should hold that there just
aren't any such things as properties and
their ilk. There are concrete objects—
God, persons, material objects—but no
abstract objects. There are red houses

and red sunsets, but no such thing as the property of being red; there may be five chairs and three dogs in the room, but no such thing as the number three or the set of dogs or the proposition *there are three dogs in the room.*

2. The Nature of Simplicity

But of course this is not the conclusion Aquinas draws; he argues that in some way all these things are identical with God. God is identical with his properties and with his essence. The latter, further-more, is in some obscure way identical with the Divine Ideas, among which are to be found properties, kinds, and exem-plars. What Aquinas says on this head (ST, Ia, 15; SCG I, 51-54) is desperately difficult; but the conclusion is that the whole Platonic realm is identical with God's essence and thus with God himself. How this is to be construed I do not know; it is far from clear that this is com-patible with the obvious fact that, for example, the property of being a horse is distinct from that of being a turkey and

both are distinct from God and his
essence. But suppose we turn from the
Platonic swarm to consider those properties God himself exemplifies; here divine
simplicity is on strongest ground. Aquinas develops this doctrine by denying
various salient kinds of complexity of
God. He is not composed of extended
parts (he is not a physical object); he is
not composed of form and matter; there
is no composition of substance and
nature in him—that is, he is identical
with his nature; there is no composition
of nature and existence in him, nor of
genus and difference, or substance and
accident or potentiality and actuality (ST
Ia, 3, 1-7). Aquinas adds that God is
identical with goodness itself and with
his goodness (SCG I, 38), with his act of
understanding (SCG I, 45), his will (SCG
I, 73) and his justice (ST Ia, 21, 1, ad 4).
Now some of these claims are quite
unproblematic. Everyone (with the
possible exceptions of David of Dinant
and Thomas Hobbes) agrees both that
God is immaterial—not a physical or
material object—and that He has no

body. Accordingly, there is no composition of spatial parts in him; nor is there composition of matter and form in him, if, as seems plausible, an object contains matter only if it is a material object.

The claim that there are no accidents in God is more troublesome. Presumably this must be understood as the claim that God has no accidental properties. All of God's properties are essential to him; each property he has is one he couldn't possibly have lacked. You and I have accidental as well as essential properties; *living in Milwaukee*, for example, is a property some of us have and have accidentally. *Being a bit corpulent* is a property Aquinas is alleged to have had, and one he could have lacked. But all of God's properties are essential to Him.

What are Aquinas' reasons for holding that all of God's properties are thus essential to him? One reason—the one presently relevant—perhaps goes as follows. If God had a property P accidentally—had it but could have lacked it— then he could not be identical with P. For suppose he were identical with P.

Then it would be impossible that he exist
and be distinct from *P*; if an object *x* is
identical with an object *y*, then *x* is essentially identical with *y*. But by hypothesis
he could have existed and not had *P*. So
he could have existed and been identical
with a property that he didn't even have.
So if he were identical with *P*, then it
would be possible that he be identical
with a property he didn't have. But that
is clearly *not* possible. Accordingly, God
is not identical with any property accidental to him. But then if he has an accidental property, there is something
distinct from him that limits and conditions him; for then he could not be the
way he is if that property did not exist.
Hence each property he has must be
essential to him.

Now if we take the term 'property' in
the very broad sense presently custom-
ary, this is of course paradoxical and
plainly false. In that broad use of the
term, one property God has is *being such
that Adam sinned;* and surely this property is not essential either to Adam or to
God. Of course Aquinas would reply that

there is no such property as *being such that Adam sinned*. The singular term 'being such that Adam sinned' does not denote a property, and the open sentence '*x* is such that Adam sinned' while it has true substitution instances, does not express a property. One who asserts that God is such that Adam sinned speaks the truth, no doubt, but does not predicate a property of God. This response is plausible. In claiming that God has no accidents, Aquinas meant to make no claims at all about *being such that Adam sinned*. As we have seen, his reason for holding that God has no accidental properties is that if he did, then he would be dependent for being the way he is, for being what he is like, upon some object distinct from him. But *being such that Adam sinned* doesn't really characterize God, so that he couldn't plausibly be said to be dependent upon it for being the way he is. *Being such that Adam sinned* is relevant to the way *Adam* is; it has nothing to do with God's being the way *he* is.

But what about such alleged properties as *having created Adam* and *knowing that Adam sinned*? Aren't these properties God has, and isn't it possible that he should have lacked them? Aquinas' answer here, I think, would be the same as in the previous case; 'having created Adam' and 'knowing that Adam sinned' do not denote properties. It is of course true that God has created Adam and true that God knows that Adam sinned; but one who affirms these propositions predicates no property of God. *God has created Adam* signifies a *relation*—a relation that is to be found in Adam but not in God. A real property of God, unlike *having created Adam* will be *non-relational*.

I think this reply leaves a good deal to be desired. In essence Aquinas (as I am representing him) rejects the claim that God has accidental properties by denying that such items as *having created Adam* or *knowing that Adam sinned* are properties. I can't see that this is helpful; for even if *having created Adam* isn't a *property* it is at any rate something that *characterizes* God, and it is something

such that its characterizing him makes
him different from what he would have
been had it not characterized him. It
seems plainly mistaken to say that the
proposition *God created Adam* characterizes Adam but not God or says
something about the former but not the
latter. If I know that God created Adam,
then I know something about God as
well as Adam; I know that he has the
attribute or characteristic of having
created Adam. Whether we call this
characteristic a 'property' or not is really
of no consequence; if it isn't a property it
is at any rate very much like a property.
And among God's characteristics, we
will find some that he could not have
lacked and some (*having created Adam*,
e.g.) that he could have. We needn't call
this a composition of essence and accident, but the distinction remains: some
of God's characteristics characterize him
in every possible world and some do not.
And if there is something objectionable,
from the point of view of the sovereignty-
aseity intuition, in God's having both
essential and accidental properties, there

will be something equally objectionable
in his having two kinds of characteristics:
those he couldn't have lacked and those
he could have. But suppose we waive this
difficulty for the moment.

The question of actuality-potentiality
complexity inherits all the difficulty con-
nected with essence-accident complexity
and is furthermore vexed in its own
right. Just as it seems right to suppose
there are characteristics God has but
could have lacked, so it seems right to
think there are characteristics he lacks
but could have. It is natural to think, furthermore, that among these there are
some he hasn't yet acquired but could ac-
quire. No doubt he hasn't yet created all
the persons he will create; he will create
persons distinct from all those that have
so far existed. If so, there is at least one
individual essence E such that God does
not now but will have the characteristic
of causing E to be instantiated. If so, he
is in potentiality with respect to that
characteristic.

Here, of course, things are compli-
cated by Aquinas' doctrine of God's eter-

DOES GOD HAVE A NATURE?

nity or timelessness. He holds that God is not in time at all; then presumably it isn't correct to say that he hasn't yet caused E to be exemplified, but will do so at some future time. This is a large and complex question.[7] Here I shall say only that I think Aquinas, in company with much of the theistic tradition, is mistaken in taking God to be thus timeless. God's life is of endless (and beginningless) duration; he has always existed and always will. His knowledge, furthermore, is not temporally limited; he knows the future in the same minute detail as he knows the present and the past. But to add that he is somehow timeless, somehow not in time at all, is to court a host of needless perplexities. There is nothing in Scripture or the essentials of the Christian message to support this utterly opaque addition, and much that seems *prima*

---

7. N. Wolterstorff unravels some of the complexities in "God Everlasting" in *God and The Good* (ed. C. Orlebeke and L. Smedes). Grand Rapids: Eerdmans, 1975.

facie to militate against it. God spoke to Abraham and did so, naturally enough, during the latter's life time. God created Adam and Eve and did so well before he created, say, Bertrand Russell. God led the children of Israel out of Egypt; he did so after he created Abraham and before he spoke to Samuel. On the face of it, then, God acts in time, acts at various times, and has done some things before he did others. It is at best Quixotic to deny this *prima facie* truth on the tenuous sorts of grounds alleged by those who do deny it.

Potentiality-actuality complexity, therefore, raises deep and difficult questions. Rather than pursue them here, let us turn to the most important and most perplexing denial of divine composition: the claim that there is no complexity of properties in him and that he is identical with his nature and each of his properties. God isn't merely good, on this view; he is goodness, or his goodness, or goodness itself. He isn't merely alive; He is identical with his life. He doesn't merely have a nature or essence; he just *is* that nature, is the very same thing as it is. And this is a hard saying. There are two difficulties, one substantial and the other truly monumental. In the first place if God is identical with each of his properties, then each of his properties is identical with each of his properties, so that God has but one property. This seems flatly incompatible with the obvious fact that God has several properties; he has both power and mercifulness, say, neither of which is identical with the other. In the second place, if God is identical with each of his properties, then, since each of his properties is a property, he is a property—a self-exemplifying property. Accordingly God has just one property: himself. This view is subject to a difficulty both obvious and overwhelming. No property could have created the world; no property could be omniscient, or, indeed, know anything at all. If God is a property, then he isn't a person but a mere abstract object; he has no knowledge, awareness, power, love or life. So taken, the simplicity doctrine seems an utter mistake.

But perhaps we can take it another way. Aquinas also says of God, not that he is identical with *life*, but that he is identical with *his* life. Perhaps the idea is that God is identical, not with power and knowledge, but with *his* power and *his* knowledge. The view would thus imply, not indeed that power and knowledge are identical, but that they are, we might say, identical in God; his knowledge is identical with his power. His essence or nature, furthermore, would be identical with his knowledge and power; but (where 'E' names his essence) E is identical neither with knowledge nor power. How can we understand this? Perhaps as follows. Suppose we consider Socrates and wisdom: we can distinguish Socrates from wisdom and each of them from the state of affairs *Socrates' being wise*—a state of affairs that obtains or is actual if and only if Socrates displays wisdom. Perhaps we could refer to *Socrates' being wise* by the locutions 'Socrates' having wisdom' or 'the wisdom of Socrates' or even 'Socrates' wisdom.' And when Aquinas speaks of God's life or

God's wisdom, perhaps we may take him as speaking of the states of affairs consisting in God's being wise and having life. Then his simplicity doctrine could be construed as making the following claim:

(3) For any properties P and Q in God, *God's having* P is identical with *God's having* Q and each is identical with God.

More plausibly, since Aquinas never spoke of states of affairs, perhaps *we* might try thus to outline a sensible defense of a simplicity doctrine similar to his.

This suggestion is indeed of some help with respect to the first difficulty I mentioned above. For while it is obviously absurd to claim that wisdom and power are the very same property, it is not obviously absurd to hold that *God's being wise* is the same state of affairs as *God's being powerful*. If, as Aquinas holds, God is *essentially* wise and *essentially* powerful—is wise and powerful in every possible world in which he exists—then the states of affairs *God's being wise* and

God's being powerful are equivalent in
the broadly logical sense: they obtain or
are actual in the very same possible
worlds. Several philosophers hold that
propositions are identical if equivalent in
this sense; they hold that if propositions
A and *B* are logically equivalent, i.e.,
true in the same possible worlds, then *A*
is identical with *B*. And if this can be
held with some show of plausibility for
propositions, then surely the same goes
for states of affairs. And if you think this
can't plausibly be held for propositions,
take heart; we can tighten up the relevant criterion of identity as follows:

(4)   States of affairs *x's having P* and *y's
      having Q* are identical if and only if
      x's having P is equivalent to (obtains
      in the same possible worlds as) *y's
      having Q* and $x = y$.

On this criterion *God's having power* is
identical with *God's having wisdom* and
(where 'E' names God's essence) *God's
having E*. Each of the mentioned properties is essential to him, so that he has each
of these properties in every possible
world in which he exists; hence the men-

tioned states of affairs obtain in the same possible worlds and are thus equivalent. True, this criterion has a mildly annoying consequence with respect to Socrates: his having P and his having Q will be the same state of affairs for any properties P and Q essential to him. Thus *Socrates' being a person*, *Socrates' being a non-number* and *Socrates' being self-identical* will be the very same state of affairs. But this consequence is only mildly annoying, and perhaps we can accept it with a certain equanimity. This version of the simplicity doctrine can thus be defended against the first sort of objection.

Still, the view in question is totally unsatisfactory. First, it does not resolve the difficulty the simplicity doctrine was invoked to resolve. The underlying motivation for that doctrine was to provide a way out of the dilemma whose horns were: either God has no nature or else God isn't genuinely sovereign. The simplicity doctrine aims to escape between the horns by holding that God has a nature and properties, all right, but they aren't distinct from him, so that he cannot rightly be said to be limited by something distinct from himself. But on the present suggestion, he does have a nature and properties distinct from him. On this view, God is identical with a certain state of affairs; even so, on the view in question, he has essentially such properties as goodness and knowledge and is distinct from them. Since they are essential to him, furthermore, they exist in every world he does. But Aquinas holds that God is a necessary being; he exists in every possible world. If so, the same must be said for these properties. But then how can they be dependent on him? That they exist and have the characteristics they have is not up to him. And won't he be dependent upon them for his nature and character? The dilemma remains untouched.

Second and more important: on this view God is a state of affairs. If he is identical with his being wise, for example, then he is the state of affairs consisting in God's being wise. And this is every bit as outrageous as the claim that God is a property. If God is a state of

affairs, then he is a mere abstract object
and not a person at all; he is then without
knowledge or love or the power to act.
But this is clearly inconsistent with the
claims of Christian theism at the most
basic level.

So initially, at least, it looks as if
Aquinas means to suggest that God is
identical with some property or perhaps
with a certain state of affairs. Both of
these suggestions are eminently reject-
able. What Aquinas says here, however,
is at times terse and enigmatic; perhaps I
haven't completely understood him. Perhaps when he argues that God is identical with his essence, with his goodness,
with goodness itself, and the like, he
doesn't mean to identify God with a
property or state of affairs at all, but
with something quite different. If so, it
isn't easy to see what sort of thing it
might be. Taken at face value, the
Thomistic doctrine of divine simplicity
seems entirely unacceptable. Like the
view that our concepts do not apply to
God, it begins in a pious and proper concern for God's sovereignty; it ends by

flouting the most fundamental claims of theism.

Or perhaps it is something else that simplicity flouts. Suppose we take a more careful look at the logic of the situation. In company with nearly all theists, Aquinas accepts

(5) God is sovereign and exists *a se* (has aseity).

He also holds

(6) God is alive, knowledgeable, capable of action, powerful and good,

a proposition essential to any brand of theism. In addition, I think he means to endorse

(7) If (5), then (a) God has created everything distinct from himself, (b) everything distinct from God is dependent upon him, (c) he is not dependent on anything distinct from himself, and (d) everything is within his control.

(7) is what we have been calling the

"sovereignty-aseity intuition"; it lays down allegedly necessary conditions of the conjunction of sovereignty with aseity. Furthermore, I think Aquinas accepts

(8)   If (6), then there are such properties as life, knowledgeability, capability of action, power and goodness; and God has these properties.

Now Aquinas speaks, not of God's *having* properties, but of properties being *in* God; he thinks of God's properties as *constituents* of Him. There is a difference between thinking of God as *having* properties and thinking of his properties as *constituents* of him. In some contexts this difference may be significant and we must bear it in mind. Here, however, I think it is not significant, and for ease of exposition I shall use 'having properties' to cover having properties as constituents. Aquinas also endorses, I believe, all of the following:

(9)   If God has properties distinct from him, then he is dependent on them.

(10)   God is a necessary being.

(11) God is essentially alive, knowledge-
      able, capable of action, powerful
      and good.

(12) If (11), then there are such properties
      as life, knowledge, capability of ac-
      tion, power and goodness, and God
      could not have failed to have them.

(13) If (10) and God could not have failed
      to have these properties, then they
      could not have failed to exist, are
      necessary beings.

(14) If God has some properties that exist
      necessarily and are distinct from
      him, then God is dependent on these
      properties and they are independent
      of him, uncreated by him and out-
      side his control.

Aquinas accepts all of these propositions, I think; and together they entail
that God's properties are not distinct
from him. In fact they entail this at least
twice over; (5)-(9) entail this conclusion
as do (5) and (7) together with (10)-(14).
And as I have argued above, all these
propositions have a certain intuitive appeal for the theist. But there are other
relevant propositions lurking in the
neighborhood—propositions that have at

least as much intuitive support:

(15) If there is a property with which God is identical, then God is a property

and

(16) No property is alive, knowledgeable, capable of action, powerful or good.

(15) is a truth of logic; and (16) seems very secure. If God is a living, conscious being who knows, wills and acts—if, in a word, God is a *person*—then God is not a property or state of affairs or set or proposition or any other abstract object.

Someone might object that our language about God, according to Aquinas, is *analogical* rather than univocal, so that when we predicate 'being a property' or 'being identical with his nature' of God, what we say doesn't mean the same as when we predicate these things of other beings. He might add that since this is so, we cannot properly draw the above inferences; we cannot properly claim, for example, that if God is a person, then he is not a property or state of affairs. The sentences 'Socrates is a person' and 'Socrates is a property (or state

of affairs)' express incompatible propositions; but 'God is a person' and 'God is a
property (or state of affairs)' do not—or
at any rate we have no reason to suppose
that they do. Since our language about
God is merely analogical, we cannot rely
on the usual sorts of inferences in talking
and thinking about God.

The teaching that our language about
God is analogical rather than literal is
another large and difficult topic—one I
cannot discuss here. What is crucially
important to see, however, is that the
present objection is a two-edged sword.
The claim is we cannot rely on our usual
styles of inference in reasoning about
God; hence we can't object to the simplicity doctrine by arguing that *God is a
person* entails *God is not a property*. But
if this claim is true, then we are equally
handicapped when it comes to the arguments *for* divine simplicity. If we can't
rely on our usual modes of inference in
reasoning about God, by what right do
we argue from (5)-(9), say, to the conclusion that God is not distinct from his
properties? Suppose it is a fact that our

language about God is analogical: if that fact vitiates the argument *against* divine simplicity, it pays the same compliment to the arguments *for* this doctrine.

All of (5)-(16), I think, have at least some intuitive appeal for the theist. Sadly enough, we cannot accept them all; (5)-(14) entail that God is identical with each of his properties, while (6), (15) and (16) entail that God is not identical with any property at all. Thus (5)-(16) are jointly incompatible; we can't, it seems, hold to them all.

Of course there is one further possibility. Hilary Putnam has claimed that the logical law of distribution is incompatible with quantum mechanics, so that we must give up one or the other.[8] A possible course he doesn't mention is that of giving up their incompatibility; perhaps each of quantum mechanics, distribution, and the idea that incompatibles

8. "Is Logic Empirical?" in *Boston Studies in Philosophy of Science*, Volume 5 (Dordrect: D. Riedel, 1969), pp. 216-241.

can't both be true is more secure than the
claim that quantum mechanics is incompatible with distribution. Here too then;
if we are desperately attached to all of
(5)-(16) a possible course would be to reject the laws of logic according to which
(5)-(16) are jointly inconsistent. This
would be a heroic course indeed; it will
probably find few takers. But it does
highlight the main point: the point that
what we have here is a conflict of intuitions. Something has to go: either
(5)-(16) or their incompatibility. (5) and
(6), however, are non-negotiable from a
theistic point of view. (15) and (16), furthermore, each have at least as much intuitive support as any of (7)-(14). (15) is a
truth of logic and about as obvious as
anything could be. But surely (16) is
equally clear; no properties are persons.
Given (5), (6), (15) and (16), however, it
follows that (7)-(14) are not all true; the
former entail that God is not a property
and the latter entail that he is. Accordingly, we must conclude that at least one
of (7)-(14) is false. And the fact is, several
of (7)-(14) seem fairly plausible candi-

dates for that post. Is it really clear, for example, that (9) is true, that if God has properties distinct from himself, then he is dependent upon them? And what about (7), the sovereignty-aseity intuition itself? As I conceded earlier, it does have intuitive support. But (7) isn't totally easy to grasp. How, for example, are we to understand *dependence* and *control*? And is it obvious that if God is sovereign, then he has created *everything* distinct from himself—even his own properties and the fact that he has always existed? I think not. This requires further discussion and isn't obvious—not nearly as obvious, anyway, as that no properties are persons. Divine simplicity, therefore, is not the way out; for while it does indeed have a certain intuitive grounding, it scouts intuitions much firmer than those that support it.

III. Nominalism

We are therefore left with our original dilemma. We must hold either that God has a nature, which seems to run counter to the sovereignty-aseity intuition, or else we give full sway to that intuition and put up with the consequence that God has no nature at all. But initially, at least, this seems an unpalatable consequence. For if God has no nature, then no property is essential to him, so that for any property *P* he has, it is possible that he should have existed but lacked *P*. If God has no nature, he could have existed but not been omniscient; indeed, he could have existed and not known anything at all. In the same way he could have existed but been without goodness, power and life. Still further: *existence* is a property he has; but if it is not essential to him, he could have existed, but lacked it—i.e., existed and not existed. The fact is he doesn't both exist and not exist; but if he has no nature, he could have done so. He could have been both omnipotent and powerless; he could have loved his creatures and had no creatures. And all of this is hard to swallow.

1. How Shall We Construe Nominalism?

As we have already seen, however,

there is another alternative: do away
with the whole Platonic pantheon. Perhaps there aren't any properties at all, in
which case God clearly won't be dependent upon any; nor will they constitute
perplexing cases of things that he hasn't
created and are outside his control. If
there are no properties, then God will
not have any properties and thus will not
have a nature. And from this point of
view, the alleged embarrassing conse-
quences mentioned in the last paragraph
are not forthcoming. It does follow that
God has no nature and that for any property you pick, he could have existed and
lacked it (there being no properties); it
doesn't follow, however, that he could
have existed and not been omniscient, or
good, or powerful. The nominalist
doesn't hold that God is not omniscient;
indeed he is, but there's no such thing as
the property of omniscience. The truth
that God is omniscient doesn't imply that
there is some property—omniscience, for
example—that God has. Similarly, the
truth that God could not have been
without knowledge does not imply that

there is some property—knowledgeability, let's say—that he could not have
lacked. The nominalist thus rejects both
(8) and (12) above. If there are no
properties, then we can hold both that
God has no nature and that nevertheless
it is not the case that he could have failed
to be omniscient, good, powerful and all
the rest. God can be essentially omniscient even if there is no such property as
omniscience.

And while we are at it, says the nominalist, we should get rid of the rest of
that Platonic horde of propositions, states
of affairs, numbers, sets and the like—in
a word, abstract objects. These are the
real offenders; with a few exceptions (sets
with contingent members, for example)
they have always existed and exist necessarily. They are neither dependent upon
God nor created by him; and their existence and nature is not within his control.
So perhaps the truth is there are only
concrete objects—God, other persons,
and physical objects such as stars, trees
and protons. 'Concretism' would be a
more accurate if less euphonious name

for this position than the usual 'nominal-ism': the claim is that everything is a concrete object. The answer to the question 'What is there?' is 'Concrete objects.'

Of course there are several problems with this view. One that has a peculiarly contemporary ring is the following: science requires arithmetic but concretism precludes its possibility. Physicists tell us that there are only finitely many elementary particles in the universe; presumably there are only finitely many ways of combining these particles into concrete objects, so that there are only finitely many concrete objects. The theorems of arithmetic, however, will hold only if there are infinitely many objects. Nominalism is thus at variance with arithmetic. One nominalistic answer might be as follows. What physics (if accurate) shows is only that there are finitely many *material* concrete objects. But perhaps there are infinitely many *immaterial* concrete objects. Perhaps God creates an angel a week, and has always been doing so; perhaps, also, time has no beginning, so that infinitely many weeks have passed. Then by now there will be infinitely many angels. If so, the nominalist could reinstate arithmetic, and do so in the style to which we have become accustomed: the style in which one 'identifies' the natural numbers with objects—typically sets—of some kind or other. On the present view there aren't any sets, of course, but that's no real obstacle; we could identify *zero* with the angel most recently created, *one* with the next most recently created, and so on, thus bringing about a stunning *rapprochement* of arithmetic with angelology.

Not all nominalists, of course, will want to take this course; and fortunately for them there is an alternative. The nominalist can sensibly admit *sets* of contingent objects; for it is clear, I think, that such sets are just as contingent as their members.[9] Their existence, therefore, would no more compromise God's

---

9. For argument, see my paper "Actualism and Possible Worlds," *Theoria*, 1976, p. 139.

sovereignty than the existence of any other contingent, created object. Of course the nominalist will have to suppose that there isn't a set whose only member is God, no pair of sets whose only common member is God, no set whose transitive closure has him as sole member, and the like; perhaps this can be accomplished most simply by stipulating that he is not a member of any set at all.[10] On this nominalist view, then, everything there is, is either a concrete object or a set whose transitive closure contains nothing but concrete objects. And then mathematics can be developed in the usual way.

2. How Shall We Understand *Dependence?*

The argument from divine sovereignty, as I said earlier, is the best argument I know for nominalism: if God is

---

10. On the envisaged suggestion, there will be a null set only if there are a pair of non-null sets with an empty intersection; the null set, therefore, does not exist necessarily.

truly sovereign, then there are no objects independent of him and outside his control, and none on which he depends; if there are abstract objects such as properties, then there are objects independent of him, outside of his control and on which he depends; so there aren't any such objects. This may be the *best* argument for nominalism; but is it a *good* one? I think not; and to see why, we must take a closer look at the sovereignty-aseity intuition. According to this intuition, the existence of the Platonic host compromises God's sovereignty and aseity. If he has aseity, he depends upon nothing for his existence and character; and if he is sovereign, everything depends upon him. Abstract objects seem to compromise both, for they seem independent of him and he seems dependent upon at least some of them. But how shall we understand this *dependence?* What is it for one being to be dependent upon another? The fundamental notion here is of a relation between propositions or states of affairs. Los Angeles' having an adequate water supply depends upon sufficient rainfall in the Sierra—depends, that is, on there being sufficient rainfall there. Our being able to climb a snow slope on skis depends on the difference between static and kinetic friction; that is, the state of affairs consisting in there being a difference between static and kinetic friction (between ski and slope) is a necessary condition of the state of affairs consisting in our being able thus to climb. We depend upon God for our existence; that is, we depend upon God's creative and sustaining activity for our existence. More explicitly, God's acting in a creative and sustaining fashion is a necessary condition of our existing. In this last case, the necessary condition in question is a *logically* necessary condition; it is not possible, at least if traditional theism is correct, that we should exist and God not create and sustain us. In the other cases the condition in question is not logically necessary and the whole conditional is of a weaker sort. But in each case we have a state of affairs (or proposition) A dependent upon a state of affairs (or proposition) B; and the basic idea is that A is dependent upon B only if B's obtaining (or truth) is a necessary condition of A's obtaining (or truth).

In the present context, however, we are interested in what it is for one *being* to be dependent upon another being. We, for example, are dependent upon God. It is no easy task to give an accurate, informative and general account of this notion of dependence. We might initially try something like

(17) x depends upon y if and only if y's existence is a necessary condition of x's existence.

To make things a bit easier, let us restrict our attention to cases where one of the terms of the relation is God. (17) should thus be thought of as an attempt to say what it is for x to depend upon y where either x or y is God.

Dependence of one being upon another, however, is always of one being on another *for some property or feature*; we are dependent upon God for our existence, for example. So what is really involved here is x's being dependent on y

for some feature it has—its existence, let's say, or its having some other property. And when x is dependent upon y for some property P, then some state of affairs or proposition relevantly involving y is a necessary condition of x's having P. We are dependent upon God for our existence; that is, the state of affairs consisting in God's creating and sustaining us—a state of affairs crucially involving God—is a necessary condition of our existing. So perhaps we should move to

(18) x depends upon y for P if and only if x has P and some proposition or state of affairs relevantly involving y is a necessary condition of x's having P

with the same restriction on x and y as in (17). Clearly it won't be easy to say when a state of affairs *relevantly* involves an object; does *Socrates' being wise* relevantly involve wisdom? or Socrateity, the essence of Socrates? For present purposes we need not give a general answer to this question; we can stick to particular cases where the answer is clear. But even so, (18) won't do the trick. Suppose we set aside our restriction on x and y for the moment. Presumably Jim Whittaker does not depend upon Pope John Paul for his ability to climb Mt. Everest; yet the proposition

(19)   Either Jim Whittaker or Pope John Paul can climb Mt. Everest

relevantly involves Pope John Paul and is a necessary condition of Whittaker's being able thus to climb. In the same way, according to (18) God would be dependent on Bertrand Russell for the property of creating the world, since

(20)   Either God or Bertrand Russell created the world is a necessary condition of God's creating the world and relevantly involves Bertrand Russell.

We might think the problem here has to do with the fact that (19) involves Jim Whittaker as well as the Pope, and (20) involves God as well as Bertrand Russell. Perhaps (18) can be rescued by adding that the state of affairs in question involves y but not x. This won't help; presumably God is not dependent upon me for the property of having created me, but

(21)   I exist

and

(22)   I have been created

relevantly involve me, do not relevantly
involve God, and are necessary conditions of God's having created me. The
fact is some further condition has to be
added to the analysans in (18), and it
isn't at all easy to see what it might be.

One consideration, however, stands
out: it is (or was) up to God whether or
not (20), (21) and (22) are true. The state
of affairs consisting in my existing involves me (and not God); and it is indeed
a necessary condition of God's having
created me. These facts, however, don't
show that God is dependent upon me,
because it is up to him whether or not
that state of affairs obtains. He caused it
to obtain; he could have refrained from
so doing and he could, if he chose, cause
it *not* to obtain. Whether it obtains is
within his control.

The importance, for our topic, of the
notion of control can be seen from
another angle. Why not endorse an account of dependence according to which

God is clearly not dependent upon abstract objects and they clearly are dependent upon him? Why not endorse, for example,

(23) x depends upon y for P if and only if there is an action A such that y's performing A is a logically necessary condition of x's having P?

For suppose with classical theism that God is a necessary being and is essentially omniscient. Suppose, furthermore, that omniscience partly consists in being aware of and thinking about everything. Then for any abstract object O you pick, it is a necessary truth that if O exists, then God is thinking of O. God's thinking of O is accordingly a necessary condition of O's existence; and God's believing that O has some property P will be a necessary condition of O's having P. According to (23), then, abstract objects will be dependent upon God for their existence and character. Furthermore, he won't be dependent upon them for anything. No abstract object performs any actions.

Now why wouldn't a partisan of the

sovereignty-aseity intuition be prepared to accept (23) as a solution to our problem? Perhaps for the following reason. Even though God's thinking of, say, the natural numbers is a necessary condition of their existing, that they exist is not within his control; it is not as if he could refrain from thinking of them. He has not created them; there is no action he can take such that if he did, they would no longer exist; that they exist and have the properties they do is not up to him. And that means that in the relevant sense, these objects are not dependent upon him. So (23) doesn't capture the relevant sense of dependence. A reason it doesn't is that it neglects the crucial notion of control—of what is and what isn't within God's power.

There is yet a third consideration pointing to the centrality of the notion of control here. On both (17) and (18) (and any reasonably similar construals of dependence) abstract objects *are* dependent upon God—at least if traditional theism is true. For according to traditional theism God is essentially omniscient and necessarily existent. As I argued a couple of paragraphs back, if God is essentially omniscient and necessarily existent, then for any abstract object O you pick, it is a necessary truth that if O exists, then God is thinking of O. That is, God's thinking of O is a necessary condition of O's existence. According to (18), therefore, O is dependent upon God for its existence. God's existence, furthermore, is a necessary condition of God's thinking of O; hence God's existence is a necessary condition of O's existence, and O is dependent upon God according to (17). In the same way, for any property P essential to O, God's believing that O has P will be a necessary condition of O's having P. Thus O will be dependent upon God for its nature as well as its existence.

A special case of this argument applies to God's nature and any properties essential to him. If he is a necessary being and has, say, *omniscience* essentially, then it is not possible that he fail to exist and not possible that he lack omniscience. If so, it follows that necessarily, if omniscience exists, then God has it; but then omniscience is dependent for its existence upon God.

The upshot is that on (17) and (18) it isn't true that abstract objects are independent of God. And the partisan of the sovereignty-aseity intuition will construe this, I think, not as a reason for supposing that abstract objects are in fact relevantly dependent upon God, but as a reason for rejecting (17) and (18) as relevant accounts of dependence. For he will point once more to the fact that if these abstract objects are necessary beings and have their properties essentially, then that they exist is not up to God. They do not owe their existence to Him; there is nothing he can do or could have done to prevent their existence or cause them to go out of existence. In short, their existence and nature is not within God's control. And this means that they are not dependent upon God in the relevant sense—(17) and (18) to the contrary notwithstanding.

3. Dependence and Control

What all this shows, I believe, is that it

is the notion of control or up-to-ness that is central to the sovereignty-aseity intuition. As we remember, this intuition, unlike ancient Gaul, is divided into four parts: if God is sovereign and exists *a se*, then (a) he has created everything distinct from himself, (b) there is nothing upon which he depends for his existence and character, (c) everything distinct from him depends upon him, and (d) everything is within his control. But while the sovereignty-aseity intuition is thus quadrapartite, it reveals an underlying unity. What I want to suggest is that it is (d) that is really crucial, (a)-(c) being important as special cases thereof. Suppose we start with (b). As we have seen, God is not shown to be relevantly dependent upon me for his having created me by the fact that some state of affairs involving me—my existing, e.g.— is a necessary condition of his creating me; for that state of affairs is one whose obtaining is up to him. He is *relevantly* dependent upon an object *O* for his having *P* only if some state of affairs involving *O* is necessary for his having *P*, and is

furthermore such that whether it obtains
is not up to him, is not within his control.
And this helps us see why God's being
dependent upon something for having a
property *P* compromises his aseity. It
does so only because if he *is* thus dependent, then whether he has *P* is not up to
him. The state of affairs consisting in his
having *P* is then outside his control; he
hasn't caused it to be actual and it is not
within his power to abrogate it. So what
really counts here is what is or isn't
within God's control. The clear-headed
partisan of aseity will agree, I think, that
what is objectionable about God's being
dependent on something else for his
omniscience, say, is just that if he is, then
whether he is omniscient is not up to
him.

Similar considerations apply to (c).
The existence of objects relevantly independent of God compromises his sovereignty just because it is not up to him
whether or not those objects exist. God is
not responsible for their existing and displaying the character they do display;
nor is there any action he could take to

annihilate them or cause them to be differently constituted. That they exist and are thus constituted is not up to him and not within his control. And that's why their existence seems to compromise his sovereignty.

We can therefore see, I believe, that branches (b) and (c) of the sovereignty-aseity intuition are important only in that they are really special cases of (d). But the same holds for (a). The importance of the idea that God has created everything is just that for anything you pick, the fact that it exists is and was up to God and within his control. The thing exists at his sufferance and because of his free and sovereign creative activity. We must make two qualifications. In the first place, it is obviously compatible with the sovereignty-aseity intuition that God create another being who creates things, things not created by God. Obviously this situation wouldn't compromise God's sovereignty, precisely because it would still be up to God whether the subordinate creator created.

We need a second qualification. It is

natural to think that a thing has been *created* only if it has a beginning and has not existed for an infinite stretch of time. We may therefore be mildly surprised to learn that Aquinas thought it couldn't be demonstrated that the world has a beginning: "that the world did not always exist we hold by faith alone: it cannot be proved demonstratively. . . . it cannot be demonstrated that man, or the heavens, or a stone did not always exist" (ST Ia, 46). So if we think of *being created* as including *having a beginning*, then Aquinas means to argue that it cannot be demonstrated, philosophically, that the world was created. The reason, essentially, is that the sovereignty-aseity intuition does not preclude the existence of an object that was uncreated, provided that its existence is up to God and within his control. It is not incompatible with the sovereignty-aseity intuition to hold that there is an object x that (1) has existed for an infinite stretch of time and has no beginning, and (2) is caused to exist by an action God performs—an action it is within God's power to refrain from per-

forming, and such that if he did so
refrain, x would no longer exist.

We could illustrate this matter as follows. Suppose we think of the material
universe as an enormously large object
whose parts are all the other material
objects there are—all the galaxies, stars,
planets, trees, atoms and quarks. Its
parts are all the elementary particles
together with everything made of elementary particles. Suppose also that the
material universe, this large object, has
existed at any time at which there were
material objects. Suppose further, that a
material object depends, for its existence,
on God's sustaining activity; that is, a
material object exists at a time only if at
that time God sustains it in existence.
Still further, suppose it is within God's
power, at any time you pick, to refrain
from creating or sustaining in existence
any material objects at all. And finally,
suppose God has been creating material
objects for an infinite stretch of time, so
that the material universe has had no
beginning. Then clearly the universe
would satisfy condition (1) above. But it

would also satisfy condition (2); there
would be an action, namely creating or
sustaining in existence at least one material object, such that for any time t it is
up to God whether he performs it and
such that for any time t his performing it
is a necessary condition of the universe's
existing at t. And clearly it is compatible
with the sovereignty intuition that the
universe should in this sense be uncreated; for that it exists at all and that it
exists at any given time is, on this suggestion, up to God and within his control.

The central thrust of the sovereignty-
aseity intuition, therefore, is best understood in terms of the notion of control—
of what is or isn't up to God. And then it
is easy to see why the Platonic menagerie
should be objectionable. If these abstract
objects exist necessarily and have some of
their properties essentially, then that
they exist and are constituted as they are
is not up to God. There is nothing he can
do to destroy them or alter their constitution—no action he can take such that if
he took it they would no longer exist or
be constituted as they are. Similarly, we

can see why it is objectionable to suppose that he has a nature (distinct from himself); if he does, then he has many properties such that it isn't up to him whether or not he has them.

4. The Irrelevance of Nominalism

Let's say that a state of affairs S is *within God's control* if it is up to him whether or not S is actual. More exactly, where S is a state of affairs that obtains, let's say that S is *within God's control* if there is some action such that it is within God's power to take it and such that necessarily, if he did, then S would not be actual. Then the trouble with abstract objects is that if there are such things, and if they are as the realist says they are, then there are any number of states of affairs outside God's control.

Now the heroic course, as I've said, is just to forego, eschew the entire Platonic horde. If there aren't any abstract objects, there won't be any necessary beings besides God. If there aren't any abstract objects, there won't be any properties, in which case he won't have any properties essentially, in which case he will not have a nature. But in fact this course is entirely unsatisfactory. In the first place, it is just *too* heroic; there clearly *are* such things as propositions and properties. But more important in the present context, nominalism doesn't help. The nominalist, presumably, will agree that there are truths-or-false-hoods—things that are either true or false. He won't suppose, of course, that truths-or-falsehoods are necessarily existing abstract objects; he will have to construe them some other way—as utterances, or inscriptions, or perhaps set theoretical constructions from utterances and inscriptions. Now suppose we say that a truth-or-falsehood is within God's control if it is up to God whether or not it is true. More exactly, where T is a truth-or-falsehood that is true, let's say that T is within God's control if there is some action he can take—some action it is within his power to perform—such that necessarily if he were to take that action, then T would be false. Then the trouble with abstract objects, realistically construed, is that if there are such things, then there will be many truths not within God's control.

But nominalism doesn't help. We can see this as follows. Even if there are no such things as the properties of being red and being colored, it is still true and necessarily true that whatever is red is colored; that truth is not within God's control. Perhaps there's no such thing as the color red; it still won't be up to God whether it's possible that there be red things. Perhaps there's no such thing as the real number π; the truth that if a thing is π inches long, then it is more than three inches long is nonetheless not within God's power. Perhaps there's no such thing as the abstract object *all men are mortal*, or any other proposition. It remains necessarily true that if all men are mortal, then it's false that some men are not mortal; and this truth is not within God's control. Even if there is no such thing as the property *omniscience*, it remains true that God is omniscient and couldn't have failed to be omniscient, so that the truth *God is omniscient* isn't within his control.

More accurately, the question whether

these truths are within God's control, is quite independent of the question whether there are such objects as omniscience or π or colors or abstract objects generally. If there are any necessary truths and if they are pretty much the ones we think they are, then there will be about as many truths outside God's control on the nominalist view as on the realist view. The realist is committed to supposing that there are unaccountably many truths not within God's control; but the nominalist is committed to supposing there are just as many.

Or if not just as many, at any rate enough to make the difference negligible so far as the sovereignty-aseity intuition is concerned. The nominalism we envisaged (above p. 61) countenanced sets as well as concrete objects; so on that view there are as many abstract objects as you please. A more compulsive nominalist, however, might eschew sets, accepting only concrete objects. He might go on to claim that there are only finitely many elementary particles and only finitely many ways to combine them into other objects. Then there will be only finitely many truths and hence only finitely many truths not within God's control. (Of course he isn't *obliged* to think there are only finitely many truths-and-false-hoods, even if he thinks there are only finitely many elementary particles. As we have already seen, even if there are only finitely many *material* concrete objects, there may be infinitely many *immaterial* concrete objects. Perhaps God has created infinitely many angels, for example, and perhaps the nominalist can construe truths-and-falsehoods as constructions from angels and their actions—mereological sums of angels, perhaps, or constructions of some other sort.) Furthermore, this sort of nominalist must pay a high price for his pleasure in parsimony; he must give up classical mathematics.

But suppose he is willing to pay the price. On this version of nominalism there will indeed be fewer truths outside God's control than there are if realism is true. Still, the difference is negligible, so far as the sovereignty-aseity intuition is concerned. On the realist view there are uncountably many truths outside God's control; for each real number r greater than zero, for example, the truth that it is indeed greater than zero is not within God's control. For the nominalist, on the other hand, perhaps there are as few as $10^{10^{10^{10}}}$ truths outside God's control; from the point of view of the sovereignty-aseity intuition, this difference isn't worth talking about.

So far, then, the conclusion to be drawn is that nominalism is not the issue. What was originally objectionable about realism was the fact that if it is true, then there are many abstract objects independent of God on some of which he depends. What is objectionable about *that*, as we have seen, is that if there are such objects, there will be many truths not in God's control. But the latter will be the case even if nominalism is true and realism false. Nominalism thus offers no more here than realism; its initially seductive charms fade on closer inspection.

Of course the nominalist has one more

card to turn up; he may insist not just that there are no abstract objects, but that there are no necessary truths about concrete objects. For example, he may simply deny the claim that

(24)   It's false that the Taj Mahal is red but not colored

is not within God's control. He can hold that every truth is within his control. For any truth T you pick, there is an action God can perform, such that if he were to perform it, then T would be false rather than true. On this view the sovereignty-aseity intuition boasts of total satisfaction; there is nothing whatever outside the control of the Creator. There are no features of himself or anything else he must just put up with; everything whatever is and is whatever it is at his behest and by his sufferance. Thus perhaps the final refuge of nominalism is universal possibilism: the view that everything is possible.

But of course *this* option doesn't distinguish nominalist from realist; the realist can say the same thing if she sees good

reason to. She can hold that there are
abstract objects—unaccountably many,
in fact—but no truths about any of them
or about God himself that are not within
his control. They are not necessary beings and do not have any of their properties essentially. That they exist and are
the way they are is up to God. Granted,
it seems bizarre to suppose that there are
such properties as omniscience and
knowledgeability and that God can bring
it about that whatever has the former
lacks the latter; but it is no less bizarre to
think that God could cause

(25)   Any omniscient being knows some-
        thing

to be false. On this view God has no
nature—not indeed, as on nominalism,
because there are no properties, but
because there are no properties God
couldn't have lacked. God has no essential properties at all.

Nominalism, therefore, is quite irrele-
vant to the sovereignty-aseity intuition; it
does no better, here, than the most luxur-
iant Platonism. The real issue is *modal*

rather than ontological; it is a question not so much of what there is as of what God can do, what is within his control. Propositions (5)-(16) (above, p. 54-57) set our original problem. The nominalist rejects

(8)   If God is alive, knowledgeable, capable of action, powerful and good, then there are such properties as life, knowledgeability, capability of action, power, and goodness and God has these properties,

and

(12)   If God is essentially alive, knowledgeable, capable of action and good, then there are such properties as life, knowledge, capability of action, and goodness, and God has them essentially.

Rejecting (8) and (12), however, leaves us with our problem. Nominalism doesn't help. Given its own intrinsically unlovely character, therefore, nominalism is perhaps best left to the nominalists.

IV. Universal Possibilism

Nominalism, therefore, is not the real

issue; what counts is what is or isn't within God's control. What the sovereignty-aseity intuition really demands is not that there be no abstract objects, but that there be no truths about abstract objects outside of God's control. And here I must add a codicil to what was said in Part II about divine simplicity. Once we see that control is the crucial issue, we can see from another perspective the inadequacy of the simplicity solution. If there is no composition in God, then He won't have a nature distinct from himself on which he depends; but there will still be many truths outside his control. *Being red* and *being colored* will be divine ideas and in some obscure way identical with God; but the truth *whatever is red is colored* will not be within his control. In the same way, the natural numbers will be among the Divine Ideas and hence obscurely identical with God; but it will not be up to him whether or not every even number is the sum of two primes. Like nominalism, the claim that God is simple pays a high philosophical price for a doctrine that is ultimately beside the point.

The real issue, therefore, is control. What the sovereignty-aseity intuition demands is

(26)   If God is sovereign and exists *a se*,
         then every truth is within his control.

Suppose we say that God is *absolutely omnipotent* if and only if every truth is within his control—alternatively, if and only if every proposition is such that it is within God's power to cause it to be true and within his power to cause it to be false. What the sovereignty-aseity intuition requires, then, is that God be absolutely omnipotent. But if God is absolutely omnipotent, then in the first place, God will have no nature. There will be no properties he could not have lacked; for any property you pick, it is within God's power to bring it about that he lacks that property. And in the second place, there will be no necessary truths; if God is absolutely omnipotent, then *every* proposition is such that he could cause it to be false. But then every proposition could be false, so that there aren't any that are necessarily true. What the sovereignty-aseity intuition really requires, therefore, is universal possibilism.

A. Descartes And Possibilism

This implication of the sovereignty-aseity intuition was, I think, clearly evident to Descartes; there is good reason to think, moreover, that he was prepared to bite the bullet and accept the consequence that there are no necessary truths. Suppose we consider the class of truths alleged to be necessary. This class would include truths of logic, truths of mathematics, and a host of homelier items such as

(27) Red is a color,

(28) The proposition *all dogs are animals* is distinct from the proposition *all animals are dogs,*

and

(29) No numbers are persons.

Suppose we choose a name for all these truths; following Descartes, let's say these are *eternal* truths, leaving open for

the moment the question whether they
are necessary as well as eternal. Now
Descartes, clearly enough, believed that
these eternal truths were created, or instituted, or caused to be true by God's
activity:

> The mathematical truths which you call
> eternal have been laid down by God and
> depend on Him entirely no less than the rest
> of his creatures. . . . Please do not hesitate
> to assert and proclaim everywhere that it is
> God who had laid down these laws in
> nature just as a king lays down laws in his
> kingdom.[11]

> As for the eternal truths, I say once more
> that *they are true or possible only because*
> *God knows them as true or possible. They*
> *are not known as true by God in any way*
> *which would imply that they are true inde-*
> *pendently of Him.* If men really understood
> the sense of their words they could never
> say without blasphemy that the truth of
> anything is prior to the knowledge which

11. Letter from Descartes to Mersenne, April 15, 1630.
In *Descartes Philosophical Letters*, tr. and ed. by
Anthony Kenny (Oxford: at the Clarendon Press,
1970), p. 11.

God has of it. In God willing and knowing
are a single thing in such a way that *by the
very fact of willing something he knows it
and it is only for this reason that such a
thing is true.* So we must not say that if *God
did not exist nonetheless these truths would
be true;* for the existence of God is the first
and the most eternal of all possible truths
and the one from which alone all others
derive (To Mersenne, May 6, 1630).

You ask me *by what kind of causality God
established the eternal truths.* I reply: *by
the same kind of causality* as he created all
things, that is to say, as their *efficient and
total cause.* For it is certain that he is no less
the author of creatures' essence than he is of
their existence; and this essence is nothing
other than the eternal truths. I do not conceive them as emanating from God like rays
from the sun; but I know that God is the
author of everything and that these truths
are something and consequently that he is
their author (To Mersenne, May 27, 1630).

It is because He willed the three angles of a
triangle to be necessarily equal to two right
angles that this is true and cannot be otherwise; and so in other cases.[12]

To one who pays attention to God's immensity, it is clear that nothing at all can exist
which does not depend on Him. This is true

not only of everything that subsists, but of
all order, of every law, and of every reason
of truth and goodness; for otherwise God,
as has been said just before, would not have
been wholly indifferent to the creation of
what he has created (Reply to Objections
VI, p. 250).

It is therefore plain that on Descartes'
view God has instituted, caused, au-
thored or created the eternal truths.
His reasons for saying so would extend
beyond these truths to allegedly necessary beings generally—to all the abstract
objects such as properties, numbers,
propositions, states of affairs, possible
worlds and the like.[13] It doesn't obviously
follow from what he says, however, that
there was a time when abstract objects
did not exist or that they had a begin-

---

12. Reply to Objections to Meditation VI, in *The
    Philosophical Works of Descartes*, tr. E. Haldane
    and G. Ross (Cambridge: at the University Press,
    1967) Vol. II, p. 250.

13. . . . I know that God is the author of everything
    and that these truths are something and conse-
    quently that he is their author." Descartes to
    Mersenne, May 27, 1630.

ning. Descartes suggests that God's insti-
tuting or causing these things consists in
his willing them—perhaps *affirming*
them:

> You ask what God did in order to produce
> them. I reply that from all eternity he
> willed and understood them to be, and by
> that very fact he created them (To
> Mersenne, May 27, 1630).

Perhaps for any Platonic entity you pick
and any time, at that time God was
affirming that Platonic entity. In the case
of numbers and properties, what he affirms is their *existence;* in the case of eternal truths what he affirms is both their
existence and their *truth.*

According to Descartes, then, God
establishes the eternal truths, and they
are dependent upon him for their existence and properties. This suggests that it
was within God's power to *refrain* from
affirming the eternal truths, so that he
could have brought it about that they
should not have been true. It suggests
that it was within God's power to cause
them to be false, causing their negations
to be true. But if God could have done

this, then the eternal truths could have been false; and if they could have been false, then they aren't necessary.

1. Did Descartes Accept Universal Possibilism?

This is, did he hold that in fact the eternal truths are *not* necessary? Several passages suggest that he did:

> You ask also what necessitated God to create these truths; and I reply that just as He was free not to create the world, so He was no less free to make it untrue that all the lines drawn from the centre of a circle to its circumference are equal. And it is certain that these truths are no more necessarily attached to his essence than other creatures are *(Loc. cit.)*.

> I turn to the difficulty of conceiving how it was free and indifferent for God to make it not be true that the three angles of a triangle were equal to two right angles, or in general that contradictories could not be true together. It is easy to dispel this difficulty by considering that the power of God cannot have any limits, and that our mind is finite and so created as to be able to conceive as possible things which God has wished to be in fact possible, but not to be able to conceive as possible things which

God could have made possible, but which he has in fact wished to make impossible. The first consideration shows us that God cannot have been determined to make it true that contradictories cannot be true together, and therefore that he could have done the opposite (To Mesland, May 2, 1644).

Again it is useless to inquire how God could from all eternity bring it about that it should be untrue that twice four is eight, etc.; for I admit that that cannot be understood by us. Yet since on the other hand I correctly understand that nothing in any category of causation can exist which does not depend upon God, and that it would have been easy for Him so to appoint that we human beings should not understand how these very things could be otherwise than they are, it would be irrational to doubt concerning that which we correctly understand, because of that which we do not understand and perceive no need to understand (Reply to Objections VI, p. 251).

These passages pretty clearly teach that it was (and is) within God's power to bring it about that such eternal truths as $2 \times 4 = 8$, and *the sum of the angles of a triangle = 2 right angles* should have

been false. And if God could have
brought it about that $2 \times 4 = 8$ should
have been false, then $2 \times 4 = 8$ could
have been false and is not necessarily
true. What these passages seem to teach,
therefore, is that there are no necessary
truths at all; every truth is contingent.
Suppose we call this view 'universal possibilism.' This is a puzzling and peculiar
doctrine indeed. Among our most stable
modal intuitions are that such propositions as

(30) $2 \times 4 = 8$

(31)   It's not the case that all men are mor-
        tal and some men are not mortal

(32)   It's not the case that God has created
        creatures that He has not created

could not have been false; their falsehood
is impossible, in the broadly logical[14] or
metaphysical sense, and there neither is
nor could have been a being within
whose power it was to cause them to be

---

14. See my book *The Nature of Necessity* (Oxford: Ox-
    ford University Press, 1974) Chapter I.

false. As Descartes says, "It is useless to inquire how God could from all eternity bring it about that it should be untrue that twice four is eight, etc., for I admit that that cannot be understood by us" (*Loc. cit.*).

2. Did Descartes Accept Limited Possibilism?

The fact is in some of the very same passages and elsewhere Descartes seems to make a quite different suggestion: he suggests that while the eternal truths are indeed necessary, it is God who has made them so and he could have made them contingent instead. Call this view 'limited possibilism.' Peter Geach sees Descartes as teaching limited possibilism, at least with respect to the truths of logic and mathematics:

> Descartes held that the truths of logic and arithmetic are freely made to be true by God's will. To be sure, we clearly and distinctly see that these truths are necessary; they are necessary in our world, and in giving us our mental endowments God gave us the right sort of clear and distinct ideas to see the necessity. But though they are necessary, they are not necessarily necessary; God could have freely

chosen to make a different sort of world, in
which other things would have been
necessary truths.[15]

There are passages that confirm this interpretation; for example,

I turn to the difficulty of conceiving how it
was free and indifferent for God to make it
not be true that the three angles of a
triangle were equal to two right angles, or
in general that contradictories could not be
true together. It is easy to dispel this difficulty by considering that the power of
God cannot have any limits, and that our
mind is finite and so created as to be able to
conceive as possible things which God
could have made possible, but which he has
in fact wished to make impossible. The first
consideration shows us that God cannot
have been determined to make it true that
contradictories cannot be true together,
and therefore that he could have done the
opposite. The second consideration shows
us that even if this be true, we should not
try to comprehend it since our nature is
incapable of doing so. And even if God has
willed that some truths should be necessary,
this does not mean that he willed them

----

15. *Providence and Evil* (Cambridge: Cambridge
University Press, 1977), pp. 10-11.

necessarily; for it is one thing to will that they be necessary, and quite another to will them necessarily, or to be necessitated to will them. I agree that there are contradictions which are so evident, that we cannot put them before our minds without judging them entirely impossible, like the one which you suggest: that *God might have made creatures independent of him.* But if we would know the immensity of his power we should not put these thoughts before our minds (To Mesland, May 2, 1644).

and

Thus, to illustrate, God did not will to create the world in time because he saw that it would be better thus than if he created it from all eternity; nor did he will the three angles of a triangle to be equal to two right angles because he knew that they could not be otherwise. On the contrary . . . it is because he willed the three angles of a triangle to be necessarily equal to two right angles that this is true and cannot be otherwise; and so in other cases.[16]

We are not "able to conceive as possible things which God could have made

---

16. Reply to Objections to Meditation VI.

possible, but which he has in fact wished
to make impossible;" "it is because he
willed the three angles of a triangle to be
necessarily equal to two right angles that
this is true and cannot be otherwise . . ."
These passages clearly suggest that some
things are impossible and other things
necessary—that the three angles of a triangle be equal to two right angles, for
example. These passages clearly suggest,
further, that it is up to God which truths
are necessary; he could have brought it
about that the three angles of a triangle
are *not* necessarily equal to two right
angles.

Accordingly, Descartes makes two
quite distinct suggestions about eternal
truths: universal possibilism and limited
possibilism. It isn't at all obvious that
Descartes clearly distinguished these two
suggestions, and the way he runs them
together in the same passage suggests
that he did not. In the next to last quoted
passage, for example, Descartes appears
to say that in fact God has wished to
make some things impossible (though he
could have made them possible). He also

seems to say, however, that God could have made contradictories true together; and, in the same letter, he adds

Just as God was free not to create the world, so he was no less free to make it untrue that all the lines drawn from the center of a circle to its circumference are equal.

So perhaps Descartes wasn't clear that there are two distinct suggestions here. Or perhaps what he means by 'necessary' and 'impossible' isn't quite what *we* mean by those terms; perhaps he sometimes uses 'necessary' as a synonym for 'eternal.'

In any event it is obvious that there are two quite separate suggestions here. Suppose we take both suggestions to concern all eternal truths, not just those of logic and mathematics. According to universal possibilism, the first suggestion, there are no necessary truths and no impossible falsehoods; everything, every proposition, is possible because God could have made it true. According to limited possibilism on the other hand, it is true and cannot be otherwise that the three angles of a triangle are equal to two right

angles; and there are things—"that contradictories cannot be true together," for
example—which "God could have made
possible but which he has in fact wished
to make impossible." On this suggestion,
therefore, there are both necessary and
impossible propositions. Thus

> (33)   God has created Descartes, but Des-
>   cartes has not been created

is in fact impossible; hence not even God
could have made it true. God could have
done something else, however; he could
have made (33) *possible*. God made (33)
impossible and he could have made it
possible. On this suggestion, there are
indeed necessary and impossible propositions; but *modal* propositions—propositions, which, like

> (34)   It is impossible that God has created
>   Descartes and Descartes has not been
>   created

ascribe a modality to another proposition—are all contingent. According to
universal possibilism,

> (35)   Possibly *p*

is true for every proposition *p*; according to limited possibilism, on the other hand, (35) is false, but

(36)   Possibly possibly *p*

is true for every *p*. On this suggestion, God affirms

(30) $2 \times 4 = 8$

in every possible world; and in the actual world he affirms

(37)   Necessarily, $2 \times 4 = 8$.

However, there are worlds in which He does not affirm (37): worlds such that if they had been actual, then *there would have been* possible worlds in which God does not affirm (30). In fact there are no such possible worlds; but God could have brought it about that there were some.[17]

---

17. In terms of the accessibility relation of modal logic: God affirms (30) in every world accessible from the actual world. There is a possible world *W*, however, in which he does not affirm (37), (affirming its denial instead): and if *W* had been actual, then there *would have been* a possible world *W** in which God affirms the denial of (30).

3. Possibilism and Control

The textual evidence, therefore, is a bit ambiguous. Nevertheless perhaps we can ask and answer this question: which of these two suggestions would fit better with Descartes' basic view of the subject? Which would he have preferred, had he clearly distinguished them? Descartes' central claim here is that God's power and freedom must be infinite, i.e., without limits; "the power of God," he says, "cannot have any limits." Why does he think God's power cannot have any limits? Because, I suggest, he believes that God is the sovereign first being of the universe on whom *everything* depends, including the eternal truths:

> The mathematical truths which you call eternal have been laid down by God and depend on Him entirely no less than the rest of his creatures. Indeed, to say that these truths are independent of God is to talk of Him as if He were Jupiter or Saturn and to subject Him to the Styx and the Fates (To Mersenne, April 15, 1630).

Elsewhere he adds that the eternal truths "are true or possible only because God knows them as true or possible. They are not known by God in any way that would imply that they are true independently of Him" (To Mersenne, May 6, 1630). They are dependent upon God, first, for their existence: "You ask what God did in order to produce them. I reply that from all eternity he willed and understood them to be, and by that very fact he created them" (To Mersenne, May 27, 1630). But they are also dependent upon God for their *truth*. And here, I think, Descartes clearly sees what we noted in section III; the intimate connection between dependence and *power* or *control*. Descartes does not shrink from the indicated inference: if the eternal truths are genuinely dependent upon God, then they must be within his control. Each eternal truth must then be such that it was (and is) within God's power to make it false. Accordingly, God was "free to make it untrue that all the lines drawn from the center of a circle to its circumference are equal"; his power isn't limited even by the eternal truths of logic and mathematics.

The textual evidence, therefore, isn't decisive as between universal and limited possibilism, although I believe it favors the former. When we consider the fundamental thrust of Descartes thought, however, the former interpretation seems clearly superior. Descartes means to hold that *everything* is dependent upon God. But then the eternal truths are thus dependent. He sees further that if they are dependent upon God, then they are within his control; he could have made them false. According to limited possibilism, *modal* propositions—propositions that ascribe a modality to another proposition—are within God's control; it is up to him whether a proposition is necessary, contingent, or impossible. The eternal truths themselves, however, are not within God's control. On this interpretation, God could not have made

(30) $2 \times 4 = 8$

false; what he could have done is only this: he could have made it the case that he *could have* made (30) false. He could have made it *possibly* false. But this is at most a trifling and churlish concession to Descartes' deep conviction that *all* things are dependent upon God and hence within his control. What he really meant to say, I think, is not just that God could have made (30) *possibly* false; he could have made it *false,* and, indeed *necessarily* false.

And here Descartes is not speaking just of mathematical truths; he means to say, I think, that *all* truths are within the control of God. For example, God could have made

(33)   God has created Descartes, but Descartes has not been created

true. He could have made "contradictories true together." *Every* truth is within his control; and hence no truth is necessary.

Descartes concedes that there is a problem here: "I turn to the difficulty of conceiving how it was free and indifferent for God to make it not be true that the three angles of a triangle were equal to two right angles, or in general that contradictories could not be true together." The difficulty is that some propositions seem obviously impossible; we cannot entertain them without judging them impossible: "I agree that there are contradictions which are so evident, that we cannot put them before our minds without judging them entirely impossible, like the one you suggest: *that God might have made creatures* independent of him." We are so constructed, by God, that we cannot entertain (33) or hold it before our minds without thinking it quite impossible—not just false, but impossible. The fact is, however, that it is not impossible; and if we want to know the truth here, we should *not* hold it before our minds. "But if we would know the immensity of his power, we should not put these thoughts before our minds"; for to do so is to be compelled to believe falsehood. To paraphrase Raskolnikov, if God does not exist everything is possible; according to Descartes, the same holds if God *does* exist.

B. Descartes Defended

What shall we say about Descartes'

universal possibilism? There is no denying its widespread popular appeal.
Undergraduates by the hundred have
thought it obvious that God is sovereign,
and that if he is sovereign, then everything—absolutely everything—is within
his control. And, of course, any view en-
dorsed by a philosopher as great as
Descartes has something to be said for it.
But it also has its unlovely features.
Harry Frankfurt, for example, suggests
reasons for thinking Descartes' claim—
that since God's power is infinite, no
proposition is necessary—is *unintelligible:*

> Now a person's assertion that there is
> something he cannot understand is often
> entirely comprehensible, and there may be
> quite good evidence that it is true. In the
> present instance, however, the assertion is
> peculiar and problematical. That there is a
> deity with infinite power is supposed by
> Descartes to entail the possibility of what is
> logically impossible. But if it must entail
> this, then the assertion that God has infinite
> (and hence unintelligible) power seems
> itself unintelligible. For it appears that no
> coherent meaning can be assigned to the
> notion of an infinitely powerful being as

Descartes employs it—that is, to the notion
of a being for whom the logically impossible is possible. And if this is so, then it is
no more possible for us to know or to
believe that God *has* infinite power than it
is, according to Descartes, for us to understand that power. If we cannot understand
"infinite power," we also cannot understand and hence cannot believe or know,
the proposition that God's power is infinite.[18]

But this seems incorrect. First, Descartes does not intend to say that for
God, the logically impossible is possible;
he means to say instead that nothing is
logically impossible. He does not mean to
claim that a contradiction, for example,
is logically impossible but possible for
God; he claims instead that contradictions are, in fact, possibly true because it
is within God's power to make them
true.

What someone says may be unintelligible to us in at least two ways. In the

---

18. "Descartes on the Creation of the Eternal Truths,"
   Philosophical Review, 1977, p. 44.

first place, she may utter or write strings of syllables we are unable to construe as words of any language we know. If, for example, she assertively utters "Twas brillig; and the slithy toves did gyre and gymble in the wabe," what she says is thus unintelligible. We may have a similar difficulty if instead she utters in affirmative fashion such a sentence as "The not nothings itself." Here we clearly have words of English, but they are used in such an unfamiliar fashion that we are unable to identify any proposition as the one being expressed and asserted. In both of these cases, the difficulty can sometimes be relieved; she can tell us what she means by these otherwise Delphic utterances. But what Descartes says is not unintelligible in this way. What he says, substantially, is

(38) Since God has infinite power, there are no necessary truths;

and there is no difficulty in construing these words. It's fairly clear which proposition is being asserted.

What someone says may be unintelligible to us in another way: she may

employ perfectly ordinary words in a
perfectly familiar fashion to express a
proposition which we are incapable of
grasping or understanding. Perhaps it involves concepts we don't grasp; then it
will be unintelligible to us in the way

(39)   No particle has both an instantane-
       ous position and an instantaneous
       velocity

is unintelligible to someone who doesn't
have the concepts of instantaneous position and velocity. But Descartes' claim
isn't like that either. Most of us have a
fairly adequate grasp of the concept it involves. In the passage quoted, Frankfurt
suggests that "infinite power" does not
express a concept we grasp; but this
seems wrong. God has infinite power if
and only if every proposition is within his
control—if and only if for every proposition p there is an action A he can perform, such that if he did perform A, then
p would be true. None of the concepts involved here is beyond our grasp. We can
certainly understand (38); what we cannot understand is how it could possibly

be *true*. That is, the view looks obviously false or even obviously impossible. And of course Descartes concedes this; he agrees that when we entertain such a proposition as

(40) $2 \times 4 = 7$

it looks obviously impossible. So the claim that no propositions are impossible seems itself clearly false or impossible. But this is not to say that it is unintelligible.

Shall we say that universal possibilism is *incoherent?* Incoherence is a slippery notion. Not just any necessarily false claim is incoherent; a person who holds that, say, every even number is the sum of two primes is not holding an incoherent view, even if it turns out to be necessarily false. After repeated calculations, I may believe that $26 \times 431 = 12,106$; my view is not incoherent, although it is necessarily false. What is incoherence? It may be hard to give a general answer; examples, however, are easy to come by. A theologian under the influence of Tillich or Kant might claim that there is a God, all right, but nothing whatever—not even that he exists—can be said about him. This is clearly incoherent, for here the claimant asserts that no assertions of a certain sort can be made, while his claim is an assertion of that very sort. But what Descartes says is clearly not incoherent in that way.

A theologian under the influence might also argue as follows:

(1)   God transcends human experience;

therefore

(2)   None of our concepts applies to God.[19]

But one who offers this argument is committed to supposing that our concept of transcending human experience applies to God. If so, however, the conclusion of the argument is false. Here the incoherence consists in offering an argument of such a sort that in accepting one of the premises one is committed to denying the conclusion.

---

19. See above, p. 23.

In the passage I quoted above, Frankfurt hints that Descartes has fallen into this sort of incoherence: "That there is a deity with infinite power is supposed by Descartes to entail the possibility of what is logically impossible." We could imagine Descartes arguing as follows:

(41) God has infinite power.

(42) That God has infinite power entails that no propositions are necessarily true.

therefore

(43) No propositions are necessarily true.

If Descartes offered this argument, then he would be guilty of incoherence, at any rate if he understood 'entails' in the usual fashion. For then in asserting (42) he would be committed to

(44) The proposition *if God is infinitely powerful, then there are no necessary truths* is a necessary truth

in which case his acceptance of one of the premises of his argument commits him to the denial of its conclusion. But why construe Descartes this way? Why not give him the benefit of the doubt and see him as arguing

(41)   God has infinite power;

(45)   If God has infinite power, there are
        no necessary truths;

therefore

(43)   There are no necessary truths?

All Descartes needs for the argument is
the *truth* of (45), not its necessity.

But isn't he committed to necessary
truth in offering an argument at all? The
above argument involves (is a substitution instance of) *modus ponens;* in ad-
vancing such an argument and claiming
that it is valid, isn't Descartes committed
to the necessary truth of the corresponding conditional of that argument? Must
he not suppose that

(46)   If God has infinite power and if God
        has infinite power there are no
        necessary truths, then there are no
        necessary truths

is a necessary truth? It is hard to see why.
No doubt he is committed to the *truth* of
(46); but why should he suppose it is
necessary? Of course he cannot explain
the validity of this argument in terms of

the necessity of its corresponding conditional; but that doesn't mean he cannot explain it at all. He can say, for example, that an argument is valid if it is a substitution instance of an argument form none of whose substitution instances has true premises and a false conclusion. There are problems here; but perhaps they are no more intractable for Descartes than for those contemporary logicians who give this explanation of validity. Descartes' possibilism does not compel him to give up either standard logic (first order logic with identity) or its ordinary application. He can assert the truth of all its theorems and their instances; he need only refrain from adding that they are *necessarily* true. He can accept as valid all argument proceeding in terms of standard logic; he need only refrain from claiming that their corresponding conditionals are necessary.

But how does he know that such propositions as (46) are true? Well, how do *we* know they are true? Perhaps we think we know them because we just *see* they cannot be false—because, substantially, we see that they are *necessarily* true. Descartes' retort is that what we see is not their necessity, but only their truth; and he sees that as clearly as we. God has constructed us so that we see the truth of (46) and its kin; we are so constituted that we can't help believing (46) when we entertain it. But we confuse this compulsion to believe—a fact about us and our noetic constitution—with a compulsion to be true on the part of the proposition. The fact is, says Descartes, we can't help believing (46); and we do indeed see that it is true. It doesn't follow that it is necessarily true. So he claims to know the truth of (46) in just the way everyone else does. And the rest of us, he thinks, confuse a compulsion on our part to believe such propositions with a compulsion on God's part to make them true. In all this there seems nothing in any straightforward sense incoherent.

Accordingly, Descartes' view is neither unintelligible nor incoherent. The most we can fairly say, here, is that his view is strongly counterintuitive—that we have a strong inclination to believe propositions from which its falsehood follows. This Descartes concedes; but he is unmoved. In a way, Descartes' position has more to be said for it than either nominalism or the view that God is simple. Descartes recognizes that the real issue with respect to God's sovereignty and aseity is *control*—what is or isn't within God's power. He holds that there are propositions, properties and all the rest of the Platonic swarm. He clearly sees, however, that what counts so far as these things and God's sovereignty is concerned, is the question whether or not they are within his control. He therefore holds that all the truths about these abstract objects *are* within God's control. Failing to see the centrality of control, both the nominalist and the partisan of divine simplicity misdiagnose the situation. Descartes sees the situation clearly; he sees that if we take the sovereignty-aseity intuition with real seriousness, we shall be obliged to suppose that every proposition is within God's control. But then we shall be obliged to accept universal possibilism. According to the

Reverend Andrew Mackerel, "it is the final proof of God's omnipotence that he need not exist in order to save us."[20] Descartes could concur.

V. The Divine Nature

On Descartes' view, then, God has no nature—not, indeed, because there are no properties to have, but because none of his properties is *essential* to him. There is no property he could not have lacked; if every proposition is within his control, then every proposition predicating a property of him is within his control. But then for every property P he has, there is something he could have done, some action he could have taken, such that if he had taken that action then he would not have had P. And our final question is: should we follow Descartes in giving full sway to the sovereignty-aseity intuition, thus denying that God has a nature?

---

20. Peter DeVries, *The Mackerel Plaza*, (Boston: Littl Brown and Co., 1958) p. 8.

A. A Conflict of Intuitions

The first thing we must note is that this view is indeed wildly counterintuitive. If God has no nature, then there is no property he could not have had and none he could not have lacked. So for any proposition p, God could have had the property of knowing that p. He could have brought it about, made it true, that he was powerless, without knowledge, and wicked. Indeed he could have brought it about that he was powerless, without knowledge, and wicked, but at the same time omnipotent, omniscient and morally perfect. He could have brought it about that he has a nature; and that he has a nature and furthermore doesn't have a nature. He could have brought it about that he does not exist while serenely continuing as a necessary being. He could have brought it about that we know that he exists but don't believe that he does; that we know that he exists and also know that he doesn't exist. On this view, it is logically possible, as Harry Frankfurt suggests, that God knows that he doesn't exist.

Now of course what Descartes holds is that these outrageous suggestions are possibly true, that is, not necessarily false. God could have caused them to be true. He is not holding that they may be true in the sense that for all we know they *are* true. What he says, in fact, suggests that we know they are *not* true. They are logically but not epistemically possible. Here we must ask the following question: how could we know, on Descartes' view, that these peculiar states of affairs are not actual as well as merely possible? How do we know, for example, that we don't both believe that God loves us and know that he doesn't? True, we don't believe that he doesn't love us, and we know we don't believe that; but why let that prejudice our views as to whether we know it? On the present view these things are quite compatible (since they are compatible with everything) with our both believing and knowing that he doesn't love us. And does the believer, from this point of view, have a reason for rejecting atheism? Of course he believes in God; but God could have brought it about that he both exists and doesn't exist, that theism and atheism are both true. How do we know he hasn't done just that?

It seems we can't appeal, here, to the fact that God has told us much about himself and is not a deceiver. He has told us, for example, that he loves us, and that he wishes us to love one another. On the present view, it could be both that he was entirely truthful in so saying, and that he neither loves us nor desires that we love one another. Perhaps in fact he hates us, and hopes we will follow suit by hating each other. How do we know that he doesn't?

Descartes' answer isn't entirely clear; but perhaps it would go along the following lines. God has in fact made certain propositions true and others false:

> The mathematical truths which you call eternal have been laid down by God. . . . Please do not hesitate to assert and proclaim everywhere that it is God who has laid down these laws in nature just as a king lays down laws in his kingdom (To Mersenne, April 15, 1630)

Furthermore, God has so created us that we are compelled or at least impelled to believe some of these truths. The passage continues:

> There is no single one that we cannot understand if our mind turns to consider it. They are all *inborn in our minds* just as a king would imprint his laws on the hearts of all his subjects if he had enough power to do so (To Mersenne, April 15, 1630).

He has so created us that we are impelled to believe that if he exists, then it isn't true that he doesn't exist; and we find ourselves incapable of believing that he knows that he doesn't exist, or both exists and does not exist. When we bring to mind or consider such a proposition as *2 + 1 = 3*, or *God doesn't know that he doesn't exist*, it displays a sort of luminous aura, a "clarity and brightness," to use Locke's phrase, or a sort of clarity and distinctness, as Descartes says. And when we believe a proposition that displays this aura, we may properly be said to know it. So we know that God does not both exist and fail to exist, even though that proposition is not necessarily true.

But can't the very same question rear its ugly head again? It is *possible*, Descartes says, that both

(47) God has made p true and has created in us a powerful tendency to believe p; we do believe p; and if we believe *p* we know p,

and

(48) We don't know *p* and *p* in fact is false

should be true. So how do we know that they aren't both true? Indeed, no matter what answer Descartes gives, the same question can be raised again. Descartes concedes that on his view, it is possible that

(49) $2 + 1 = 3$

should be false. So we ask: how then do you know it *isn't* false? He responds by citing some reason R. But then comes the rejoinder: you concede that it's possible that R should be true and (47) false. How then do you know that that possibility isn't *actual*?

So this question will always arise. But

does that mean that Descartes cannot
coherently claim to know that (49) is
true? I think not. How do *we* know that

    (50)   If, if p then q, and p, then q

is true? Not, presumably, by inferring it
from other propositions that are more
obvious or better known than this one;
we simply see that it is true and couldn't
be false. And why can't Descartes make
the same reply, minus the "couldn't be
false?" He doesn't know (49) or (50) on
the basis of evidence, just as the rest of us
don't. So he does not need an answer to
the question "How do you know that
those bizarre possibilities aren't actual?"
He can claim, quite properly, that he just
does know that they aren't. This objection, therefore, is inconclusive.

    The first objection, however, remains.
If Descartes is right, then every proposition is possibly true. But if we know
anything at all about modality, we know
that some propositions—

    (51)   God knows that he does not exist

for example—are impossible. Of course
Descartes concedes that "there are con-

DOES GOD HAVE A NATURE? 133

tradictions which are so evident, that we cannot put them before our minds without judging them entirely impossible, like the one you suggest: *that God might have made creatures independent of him*" (to Mersenne, May 26, 1630). He simply claims we know on other grounds that those contradictions are *not* impossible; we know this because we know that God is sovereign and omnipotent. Pared to essentials, then, his argument goes like this:

(52) God is omnipotent.

(53) If God is omnipotent, then his power is absolutely unlimited.

(54) If his power is absolutely unlimited, then he could make (51) true.

(55) If he could make (51) true, then (51) could be true and is possible.

Therefore

(56) (51) is possible.

More accurately, taking account of Descartes' seeing God's omnipotence as a consequence of his sovereignty, we could put his argument as follows:

(57)   God is sovereign.

(58)   If God is sovereign, then everything
       is dependent upon him.

(59)   If everything is dependent upon him,
       then every truth is within his control.

(60)   If every truth is within his control,
       then (51) could be true and is pos-
       sible.

Therefore

(56)   (51) is possible.

Now (57) is non-negotiable from the
point of view of Christian theism; (60)
seems utterly obvious; and both (58) and
(59) have at least some intuitive support.
As has been remarked, however, one
man's *modus ponens* is another's *modus
tollens;* (58) and (59) have at least some
support, but so does

(61)   (51) is not possible.

Indeed, (61) seems to have a good deal
more intuitive support than either (58) or
(59). Descartes' procedure here is like the
following. Suppose someone considers
the premises of a Russell paradox: that
some properties exemplify themselves

and others do not, that if so, there is such a property as self-exemplification, that every property has a complement and the like. Suppose he notes, furthermore, that each of these premises has a good deal of intuitive support and that by forms of argument themselves having strong intuitive support they entail

(62)   There is a property that both exemplifies itself and does not exemplify itself.

Finally, suppose he concludes (perhaps with an air of baffled bewilderment) that we are obliged to accept (62), despite the fact that it seems self-evidently false. Such a person has forgotten that the argument is reversible. We aren't obliged to accept the conclusion; instead we may reject one of the premises or one of the argument forms by which they entail the conclusion.

But the same goes for Descartes' argument. He thinks we should reject (61), because of (58) and (59). He concedes that we find ourselves strongly inclined to accept (61); we find it hard to see how it could possibly be false; we have a

powerful and nearly overwhelming tendency, when considering it, to accept it.
Nevertheless, we must reject it, because
its denial follows from (58) and (59). But
how could the latter have better creden-
tials than the ones just conceded to (61)?
How could they possibly have a stronger
claim on our belief? It isn't as if we are
just *given* (58) and (59) as settled in ad-
vance, while other propositions such as
(61) have no more than their intuitive
support to rely on. Descartes' reason for
supposing (58) and (59) true is just that
they seem evident upon reflection, in the
way in which it may seem evident upon
reflection that there are no things that do
not exist or that whatever has any properties exists. But of course (61) seems at
least as evident upon reflection. The
source and motivation for these conflict-
ing suggestions is the same: each seems
intuitively plausible. So what we really
have here is a conflict of intuitions. The
question is: which has stronger intuitive
support, (58) and (59) (or (53) and (54))
on the one hand, or (61) on the other? I
can't speak for Descartes, of course; but

as for me and my house, (61) seems about as stable and clear and compelling as any intuition we have—considerably more compelling than either of (58) or (59). We should therefore accept (61) and reject (58) or (59)

Could it be that a person should find herself more strongly inclined to believe (61) than (58) or (59) and nevertheless be rationally permitted or even rationally obliged to reject (61) in favor of (58) and (59)? Suppose I take the *Bible* as God's speaking to us, thereby teaching us important truths; suppose I believe

(63)   Whatever the *Bible* teaches is true.

Suppose I also believe

(64)   The Bible teaches that (61) is false;

and suppose it teaches that this powerful tendency we have to believe (61) is a result of the willfully sinful condition into which mankind has fallen. Finally, suppose that whenever I think about (61), I find myself more strongly impelled to believe it than I am to believe (63) and (64) when I think about *them*. Under those conditions, what should I do? Would I be doing the right thing in believing (63) and (64), even though they conflict with (61), which has more intuitive support than they do? To vary the case, imagine you are exploring mood and mind altering drugs; you come upon one that produces an overwhelming tendency to believe that *modus ponens* is invalid and its corresponding conditional false. You experiment widely; in 1000 out of 1000 cases the drug produces this ineluctable tendency to find *modus ponens* obviously false. You take the drug yourself. First you notice a shade of doubt creeping in about *modus ponens;* then substantial uneasiness; and after ten minutes you find yourself powerfully impelled to believe it false. It seems as improbable, to you, as any contradiction; and the more you think about it, the more obviously false it appears. Indeed, its falsehood seems much clearer and more evident to you than what you know about the drug. What should you do? I don't have the space to discuss this question (as one says when one doesn't know the answer); let me say only that it is by no means obvious that one should reject *modus ponens*, under those conditions. In the same way, it is by no means obvious that one could not sensibly reject (61) on grounds like (63) and (64), even if one has a stronger tendency to accept (61) than to accept (63) and (64).

But of course Descartes does not argue for (58) and (59) in any such fashion as this. He just takes them to be intuitively obvious. The question is: which is *more* intuitively obvious, (61), or (58) and (59)? The conflict is between two intuitions: the intuition that some propositions are impossible and the intuition that if God is genuinely sovereign, then everything is possible. But when the issue is thus baldly stated, so it seems to me, there really isn't any issue. Obviously not everything is possible; obviously, for example, it is impossible that God be omniscient and at the same time not know anything at all. And this is far more obvious than either (58) or (59). So the right course is to reject (58) or (59). We should hold that (51) is not possibly true and its denial is necessarily true. But then God has at least one essential property: not knowing that he does not exist. We should therefore assert forthrightly that God has a nature and that not everything is possible—even for him.

B. God's Nature and Necessary Beings

God has essentially the property of not knowing that He does not exist; but of course he has many more. For example, he has *existence* essentially; like everything else, he is such that he exists in every possible world in which he exists. But Christian theists have traditionally said something much stronger. Not only is it not possible that God exist but fail to exist; it is also not possible that he fail to exist. Like all the rest of us, he has existence essentially; unlike the rest of us, he also has necessary existence—the property a thing has if and only if it could not have failed to exist. There is no possible world in which God does not exist. If so, however, then the proposition

(65)   God has a nature

is equivalent to

(66)   There are some necessary proposi-
        tions.

For suppose (65) is true; then God has
essentially some property P. But then

(67)   God has P

will be a necessary truth, so that (66) is
true. Suppose on the other hand that (66)
is true. Then there is at least one
necessary proposition A. But then it follows that God has essentially the property of not knowing that A is false; hence
(65) is true. So if God exists necessarily,
the question whether he has a nature is
equivalent to the question whether there
are any necessary truths. Which properties are included in God's nature? If, as
most of the Christian tradition affirms,
he could not have been powerless, or
morally imperfect or without knowledge, then he has the complements of
those properties essentially; being knowledgeable, morally perfect, and powerful
will be part of his nature. But the tradition has typically gone further; God is
not only not possibly powerless; he is
essentially omnipotent. And not only is

he essentially knowledgeable; he is essentially omniscient. That is, he believes no false propositions, and for any true proposition p, God knows that p; and this is so in every world in which he exists. But suppose he exists in every world; then each proposition p will be equivalent to the proposition that God knows that p, which is equivalent to *God believes that p*.

Furthermore, if the number 7 or the proposition *all men are mortal* exist necessarily, then God has essentially the property of affirming their existence. That property, therefore, will be part of his nature. Indeed, for any necessarily existing abstract object O, the property of affirming the existence of O is part of God's nature. It is thus part of God's nature to say, "Let there be the number 1; let there be 2; let there be 3. . . ." According to Kronecker God created the natural numbers and men created the rest—rational numbers, real numbers, complex numbers and the like. Kronecker was wrong on two counts. God hasn't *created* the numbers; a thing is

created only if its existence has a beginning, and no number ever began to exist.
And secondly, other mathematical enti-
ties—the reals, for example—stand in
the same relation to God and humankind
as do the natural numbers. Sequences of
natural numbers, for example, are necessary beings and have been created neither by God nor by anyone else. Still,
each such sequence is such that it is part
of God's nature to affirm its existence.

And of course the same goes for other
necessarily existing abstract objects.
Though God affirms the truth of only
some propositions, he affirms the *existence* of them all; and if no proposition
could have failed to exist, then for any
proposition *p*, it is part of God's nature to
affirm that *p* exists. The same holds for
states of affairs and possible worlds; each
possible world is such that God affirms
its existence. If what is possible does not
vary from world to world, then each possible world is such that it is part of God's
nature to affirm its existence; and there is
no world in which it is part of God's
nature to affirm the existence of a world

distinct from any he does in fact affirm.
So in each possible world God affirms the
existence of the same possible worlds: the
ones that exist in fact, in the actual
world. Of course in each possible world
W he affirms the *actuality* of just one
world: W itself.[21]

From this point of view, then, exploring the realm of abstract objects can be
seen as exploring the nature of God.
Mathematics thus takes its proper place
as one of the *loci* of theology; perhaps
this explains the high esteem in which it
is held in many quarters. And the same
goes for logic, both broadly and nar-
rowly conceived. Of course God neither
needs nor uses logic; that is, he never
comes to know a proposition *A* by inferring it from a proposition *B*. Nevertheless
each theorem of logic—first order logic
with identity, let's say—is such that affirming it is part of God's nature. And to
determine that a proposition *A* is
equivalent to (i.e., true in the same

---

21. See my book *The Nature of Necessity*, Chapter IV.

worlds as) a proposition B is to determine that it is part of God's nature to believe both A or B or neither A nor B.

By way of conclusion, I wish to ask but not answer the following question. Take any necessary proposition:

(68) $7 + 5 = 12$

for example. (68) is equivalent to

(69) God believes (68);

and

(70) Necessarily $7 + 5 = 12$

is equivalent to

(71) It is part of God's nature to believe that $7 + 5 = 12$.

Can we see (71) as somehow *prior* to (70)? Explanatorily prior, perhaps? Can we explain (70) by appealing to (71)? Can we perhaps answer the question "Why is (70) true?" by citing the fact that believing (68) is part of God's nature? Can we explain the necessary existence of the number 7 by citing the fact that it is part of God's nature to affirm its existence? More exactly, is there a sensible sense of "explain" such that in that sense, (71) is the explanation of (70) but (70) is not the explanation of (71)? Or could we say, perhaps, that what *makes* (70) *true* is the fact that (71) is true? Can we ever say of a pair of necessary propositions *A* and *B* that *A* makes *B* true or that *A* is the explanation of the truth of *B*? Could we say, perhaps, that (70) is *grounded in* (71)? If so, what are the relevant senses of "explains," "makes true" and "grounded in?" These are good questions, and good topics for further study. If we can answer them affirmatively, then perhaps we can point to an important dependence of abstract objects upon God, even though necessary truths about these objects are not within his control.

Published by the Marquette University Press
Milwaukee, Wisconsin 53233
United States of America

1 St. Thomas and the Life of Learning (1937)
by John F. McCormick, S.J.
ISBN 0-87462-101-1

2 St. Thomas and the Gentiles (1938)
by Mortimer J. Adler, Ph.D.
ISBN 0-87462-102-X

3 St. Thomas and the Greeks (1939)
by Anton C. Pegis, Ph.D.
ISBN 0-87462-103-8

4 The Nature and Functions of Authority (1940)
by Yves Simon, Ph.D.
ISBN 0-87462-104-6

5 St. Thomas and Analogy (1941)
by Gerald B. Phelan, Ph.D.
ISBN 0-87462-105-4

6 St. Thomas and the Problem of Evil (1942)
by Jacques Maritain, Ph.D
ISBN 0-87462-106-2

7 Humanism and Theology (1943)
by Werner Jaeger, Ph.D., Litt.D.
ISBN 0-87462-107-0

8 The Nature and Origins of Scientism (1944)
by John Wellmuth
ISBN 0-87462-108-9

9 Cicero in the Courtroom of St. Thomas Aquinas
(1945) by E. K. Rand, Ph.D., Litt.D., LL.D.
ISBN 0-87462-109-7

#10 St. Thomas and Epistemology (1946)
by Louis-Marie Regis, O.P., Th.L., Ph.D.
ISBN 0-87462-110-0

#23 Thomas and the Physics of 1958:
A Confrontation (1958)
by Henry Margenau, Ph.D.

ISBN 0-87462-123-2

#24 Metaphysics and Ideology (1959)
by Wm. Oliver Martin, Ph.D.

ISBN 0-87462-124-0

#25 Language, Truth and Poetry (1960)
by Victor M. Hamm, Ph.D.

ISBN 0-87462-125-9

#26 Metaphysics and Historicity (1961)
by Emil L. Fackenheim, Ph.D.

ISBN 0-87462-126-7

#27 The Lure of Wisdom (1962)
by James D. Collins, Ph.D.

ISBN 0-87462-127-5

#28 Religion and Art (1963)
by Paul Weiss, Ph.D.

ISBN 0-87462-128-3

#29 St. Thomas and Philosophy (1964)
by Anton C. Pegis, Ph.D.

ISBN 0-87462-129-1

#30 The University in Process (1965)
by John O. Riedl, Ph.D.

ISBN 0-87462-130-5

#31 The Pragmatic Meaning of God (1966)
by Robert O. Johann

ISBN 0-87462-131-3

#32 Religion and Empiricism (1967)
by John E. Smith, Ph.D.

ISBN 0-87462-132-1

#33 The Subject (1968)
by Bernard Lonergan S.J., S.T.D.

ISBN 0-87462-133-X

#34 Beyond Trinity (1969)
by Bernard J. Cooke, S.J., S.T.D.

ISBN 0-87462-134-8

Uniform format, cover and binding.

Copies of this Aquinas Lecture and the others in the series are obtainable from:

Marquette University Press
Marquette University
Milwaukee, Wisconsin 53233, U.S.A.

Publishers of:
• Mediaeval
Philosophical
Texts in Translations
• Père Marquette
Theology Lectures
• St. Thomas
Aquinas Lectures